LABOR,
LAND &
LIBERTY:

A Lindy Davies Reader

Georgist Journal

134-136
2019-2021

Henry George Institute

LABOR, LAND & LIBERTY:
A Lindy Davies Reader

Georgist Journal
134-136, 2019-2021

ISBN: See back cover

Henry George Institute
4075 Cheltonham Court
Plainfield, Indiana 46168 USA

www.HenryGeorge.org
info@henrygeorge.org

Cover Design: Vajramati Minter
Cover Photo: Bristol UK. Liv Cashman Unsplash

CONTENTS

Publisher's Preface 6

Introduction by Mike Curtis 9

1 Overpopulation? No Such Thing 11

2 The Joyful Noise of Economic Justice 14

3 Building Peace 17

4 Electoral Reform 20

5 Why Are Theories of Value Important? 23

6 Political Economy and Services 30

7 Are We Disreputable? 34

8 A Georgist Stand on Corporate Privilege? 36

9 Does Georgism Have a Theory of History? 42

10 A Georgist Theory of History: Work in Progress . . . 48

11 Closing the Virtual Frontier (Redux) 63

12 Nobody's Occupying THIS Lot 71

13 Defining Political Economy 73

14 How to Break the Curse 77

15 On Fictitious Commodities, and Sacred Land 86

16 Getting It Together in Bangladesh 97

17 A Moral Structure to Address Climate Change 105

Lindy Davies (1967-2019) 111

Index 116

Understanding Economics 124

Preface

It is with both great pride and some humility that the Henry George Institute (HGI) publishes this triple issue of the *Georgist Journal* (GJ). It has been more than three years since Lindy Davies edited, designed, and released issue #133 of GJ – about a year before he, an indefatigable optimist, lost his valiant battle to cancer at the young age of sixty-one. For nearly twenty-five years Lindy had edited the GJ, a responsibility that came with the role of Program Director of HGI, a position he was groomed for by his predecessor, Bob Clancy.

It was in 1971 that HGI was founded by Bob and several of his stalwart allies from the Henry George School. Bob had already taken on the task of editing and publishing the new *IU Newsletter* on behalf of the International Union for Land Value Taxation and Free Trade. Bob worked in New York City while the IU headquartered in London: a truly international partnership. When HGI joined IU as co-publisher, the name of the periodical was changed to *The Georgist Journal*. Decades later, after a few years serving as editor, Lindy dropped "The" from the title and no one objected, if even noticed. It was a gesture of modest diplomacy on Lindy's part, since there were other Georgist journals being published.

Lindy's passing left the HGI Board of Directors with the challenge of "restarting" the Institute, including its online education problem and its Journal. But we knew of no person available to replace Lindy, especially as editor and chief writer for the Journal. After much discussion the Directors voted to publish a triple issue of GJ as a free-standing book featuring "The Best of Lindy".

Wyn Achenbaum proposed calling it *The Lindy Davies Reader*, after an earlier book that Lindy edited for HGI: *The Mason Gaffney Reader*. Realizing that many potential readers would not recognize

"Lindy Davies" (or "Georgist"), the Directors approved the descriptive title, *LABOR, LAND & LIBERTY*, with *A Lindy Davies Reader* as the subtitle. Realizing we had enough material for several volumes, we followed Lindy's example with GJ, dropping "The" – but adding "A".

"Georgist " refers to the social philosophy, economic analysis, and public policies advocated by Henry George (1839-1897), a leading Progressive reformer and author of the best-selling *Progress and Poverty* (1879). George's influence encompassed the English-speaking world and extended beyond to countries in Europe and Asia. George had a special interest in the well-being of working people. In *P&P's* analysis, in order for workers, **labor**, to secure their full and just wages, equal access to **land** (the natural world) is essential. Such access is also necessary to realize the promises of **liberty**. The goal is "association in equality"; and the way to achieve it in a monetized economy is "*To abolish all taxation save that upon land values*" (*P&P*, 1979 ed., pg. 406). This became known around the world as "The Single Tax" – with emphasis on "The", enthusiasm for "Single", and Stoic acceptance of "Tax".

Among his colleagues, Lindy was one of the most faithful to George's original vision, even as he applied it to 21st century issues. Readers not familiar with Lindy's writings have a surprising treat in store. If there is a short-cut to understanding the relevance of Henry George and "the Georgist paradigm", it is the work of Lindy Davies. This volume offers a small yet excellent sample. Lindy summed it up best, in his inimitable style, when he wrote:

"Our most important work is to teach justice. Sometimes it's appropriate, to be sure, to discuss a groovy way of invigorating cities by shifting the property tax. But we must also develop a vision. We must be able to articulate a clear, vibrant conception of what justice is and how it actually works. We must spread that message as quickly and efficiently as we possibly can; we must say it, not just over and over again because we're in the habit, but with passion. " (pp. 18-19 in this volume)

This *Lindy Davies Reader* is published thanks to the generous passion and dedication of friends and associates who donated time and talent, advice and treasure, including: Wyn Achenbaum, Polly Cleveland, George L. Collins, Lisa Cooley, Mike Curtis, Ed Dodson, Ernest Farino, Ted Gwartney, Gil Herman, Vajramati Minter, Rich Nymoen, Nicholas Rosen, Osamu Uehara, Joshua Vincent, Sue Walton – and all the loyal members of HGI.

We also acknowledge the generosity of Robert Schalkenbach Foundation. For several years, along with the IU and the Council of Georgist Organizations, RSF served as a co-sponsor of this, our *Georgist Journal.*

**In Lindy's honor and memory,
we extend our heartfelt appreciation
and dedicate this volume
to his family members,
his beloved spouse Lisa Cooley,
and their son and daughter,
Eli and Francesca Davies.**

*~ Mark A. Sullivan
Secretary
Henry George Institute
October 2021*

Introduction

For more than a century now, the United States and, for that matter, the world have grappled with the intractable problems of creating jobs, raising wages, and providing housing. For the solution, most Americans fall into one or another of two camps. One camp favors more regulations, interventions, redistributions, and government programs in varying degrees. The other camp favors just the opposite, less regulations, less interventions, less redistributions, and fewer government programs, in varying degrees. Neither group displays any understanding how the value of land accounts for the socially created wealth that could provide for government and social programs in lieu of taxes on labor and industry. This understanding is the thesis of the Gilded Age reformer Henry George in his bestselling work, *Progress and Poverty* (1879).

What you will see, in these articles by Lindy Davis, is a beautiful explanation of contemporary issues from a Georgist perspective. Lindy was not only a scholar of Henry George and Professor Mason Gaffney, but he was also well versed in the texts of micro and macroeconomics as currently taught in our colleges and universities. This was a great asset in refuting theories and presenting the Georgist prospective. As you will see, he wrote for the educated and uneducated as he went to the root cause and the Georgist solution to contemporary issues.

Lindy Davies grew up in an upper-middle-class family on the Eastern Shore of the Chesapeake Bay along the Sassafras River. I first met Lindy in the mid-1980s when he was in his mid-20s. We were working as arborists on the 150-foot-high tulip trees at the Winterthur Gardens. That is where I introduced him to the thesis of Henry George. Subsequently, he had an accident in which he seriously injured his arm. He did fully recover, but, while in the process, he went back to the University of Delaware and received master's degrees in education and literature.

Upon graduation, he was hired as the Assistant Director of the Henry George School in New York where he worked for ten years until becoming the Director of the *Henry George Institute* in1999. Lindy and his wife, Lisa, moved to rural Maine and took the Institute with them. There they built their own house and raised two children. After serving with inexhaustible devotion as the Director of the *Henry George Institute* for 20 years, Lindy died in 2019 at the age of 61.

As director of The *Henry George Institute*, Lindy Davies built and maintained the HGI website, developed numerous educational materials, conducted online correspondence courses, and obtained certification for the National College Credit Recommendation Service. He continued the correspondence courses that had been in play for decades through the post office, and took on other jobs. He was commissioned by the Robert Schalkenbach Foundation to abridge George's *Science of Political Economy* — in my opinion, a great improvement over the massive original. For HGI Lindy edited and designed *The Mason Gaffney Reader* and wrote other books, the last of which was *Understanding Economics: To Fix What's Wrong*.

Lindy is best known in the Georgist movement as the editor and publisher of the Institute's periodical, *Georgist Journal*. There he wrote many of the articles for which Georgists hold him in such high esteem. This triple issue of *Georgist Journal* constitutes *A Lindy Davies Reader* and presents a selection from what members of the *Henry George Institute* Board of Directors consider their favorite GJ articles by Lindy Davies.

Enjoy!

~ Mike Curtis
September 2020

— Chapter I —

Overpopulation?
No Such Thing

Five billion seven hundred million people is a lot of people, no doubt about it.[1] Is it too many? To an increasingly influential crew of neo-Malthusians, the answer is an emphatic YES—and their view seems reasonable at first glance, especially when fortified by such statistics as these, as published by The World Population News Service:

—600,000 square miles of forest cut in the last ten years;

—26,000,000,000 tons of topsoil lost;

—88 nations classified by the UN World Food Program as unable to provide enough food for their inhabitants;

—960 million illiterate people; 130 million children lacking access to primary schooling;

—The world's population increasing by nearly 100 million people per year.

Well, perhaps. But we know about lies, damn lies, and statistics. A hundred million people is an increase of roughly half a percentage point per year. The Earth has the capacity to absorb such numbers: Carrying capacity is the battle cry of the population alarmists, but vast capacities lie unused (or are being destroyed). Although the United States, for example, farms fewer acres every year, it always exports food and continually debates policies for handling its surplus.

Every single person in the world could have an acre of land in an area smaller than the continent of North America, at an average density of 640 people per square mile—less dense than Japan today. Africa, the poorest continent, has 20.2% of the world's land area, and 12.7% of its population. Enough arable land exists in

India to give each person in the country approximately half an acre—that's not just raw land, remember, but arable land. In famine-ravaged Ethiopia, each person could have three—quarters of an acre of arable land.

The statistics quoted above on deforestation and topsoil loss describe the consequences of land hoarding, not overpopulation. Around the world, deforestation and desertification result from peasants pushing into sub-marginal land while high-quality farmland is held out of use. The situation is so acute in Brazil, for example, that squatters have been massacred simply for occupying remote, unused areas of privately-held ranches.

Two factors consistently correlate with high birth rates: poverty and lack of education. It has long been known that when living standards rise in a community, birth rates tend to decline. Recently, however, another kind of demographic shift has been observed. Where women have had access to education and media, birth rates have showed significant declines—even though income levels had not increased.

The most distasteful part of the recent spate of neo-Malthusian cant has been the notion that irresponsible poor people should be forcibly stopped from procreating, lest their hungry numbers start to wrest control of the resources held by more civilized sorts. In an economy where more energy and resources are spent in taking pictures of children than are used to feed children in the rest of the world, this is nothing short of offensive. The richest fifth of Earth's people take in over 82% of the world's income; the poorest fifth gets less than two per cent—and these are the "irresponsible ones" that the Malthusians want to sterilize.

But wait: did I say that population growth is not a problem? Hardly—not when the world's poorest, most corrupt, most disorganized and environmentally endangered nations are the ones with the highest birth rates (of course, they have fairly high death rates as well; Africa's population actually decreased in 1996). No, there is a problem all right.

But it is time we got it straight: poverty is not caused by overpopulation. There can never be such a thing as overpopulation in a world where ample resources exist to feed every new child—but they are held idle. The miserable conditions that are misnamed "overpopulation" today are the result of poverty, not its cause.

This essay appeared as the "Land Rant" of the week for December 19, 1996 at the Institute's website. Check out our series of "Land Rants" at: http://www.henrygeorge.org

~ *Georgist Journal* #86
January 1997

End Note

1. Publishers note: As of 2021 world population is estimated to be seven billion nine hundred million.

— Chapter 2 —

The Joyful Noise of Economic Justice

Georgists can, perhaps, be excused for a certain amount of demoralization. We have been trying so hard, for so long, with such meager resources and so little to show—it's only natural that it would start to do a job on our heads. We start to believe the bad things people say about us—and even blame our lack of success on—gasp—our own faults! But it isn't so. No movement ever failed because of the inadequacies of its individual adherents! Other movements have had looser cannons and wilder shots than we have, and still carried the day.

One of my favorite pieces of advice from my favorite philosopher, Lao Tzu, is to "turn your greatest weakness into your greatest strength." It may sound paradoxical, but in fact it is the eminently practical basis for Tai Chi Ch'uan, Chinese medicine, and peace of mind generally. Let's examine some of the explanations that are offered for the Georgists' lack of success. As we do, let's consider Lao Tzu's wise advice. They say that our movement:

Is quaint and out-of-date
When you consider the level of confidence inspired by neoclassical economic theory, this becomes a stone thrown from a glass house. But *Progress and Poverty* is 120 years old, and that may make us—shall we say—unfashionable. An example: Henry George exhaustively refutes the wages-fund theory. He proves, in essence, that labor produces its own wages. Now how quaint, how archaic that idea seems, today! People work hard, as they must, to make ends meet—but any connection between the labor they perform and the reward they get seems utterly coincidental!

Today's pre-eminent economic model is that of the casino. Success, to most people, is a matter, of being in the right place at the right time. It simply isn't fashionable to suggest that another set of rules will allow everyone to win.

Lacks training and sophistication

Now, there we are hoist on the petard of our own methodology. And happily so! For one of the basic tenets of Georgist economics, sometimes downplayed, but almost as important as the land question itself, is the assertion that any thinking person can understand fundamental economics. The means to make informed decisions about economic policy are not the exclusive domain of credentialed experts! Now, is that not subversive? We may lack training in econometric gimcrackery—but if we, as Georgists, lack sophistication, we need only to apply some disciplined thought to what we know.

Is a cult

That may not be all bad! Unfortunately, though, we lack the advantage of genuine cults in being able to sleep-deprive and brainwash our converts; we have to actually convince them. Are we a small band of zealots passionately devoted to the adjustment of local property tax rates? No, we are a small band of zealots passionately devoted to the fundamental realignment of public and private economic rights in order to create a just and prosperous society. There's a difference. And anyway, the cure for being a small band of zealots is to recruit a lot more zealots. Christianity used to be a cult, too.

Disdains effective marketing techniques; refuses the advice of experts

Well, to the extent that we actually do that, it is a Bad Thing. But we don't do it as much as hawkers of high-priced marketing services would have us think. A property tax reform that promises lower taxes for most voters is easy to market. But a re-thinking of our basic right to **own land**? That's a rough one. Other movements have easy pitches to rally behind: Save the whales! Cherish the redwoods! Preserve the family farm! Make food safe! Eat the rich!

But: can you name a reform that can improve the moral, intellectual, physical quality of life, in any community, that does not depend, ultimately, on the solving of the land problem?

So, yes, our task is absurdly difficult, and there is no magic bullet to be had. But there is one other fact to consider:

Nothing Else Will Work

And that's where the joyful part comes in. If I didn't know of a solution—however difficult—to the terrifying complex of my world's problems, I couldn't face the newspapers. I would be just as avid as anyone to be anesthetized. But I don't need to hide, because I know that there is a real solution, and that, my friends, is the joyful noise of economic justice!

~ *Georgist Journal* #91
September 1999

— Chapter 3 —

Building Peace

Georgists are infamous for claiming to have the solution for everything—the single tax will cure the common cold, the boom/bust cycle, the tragedy of poor taste, the heartbreak of psoriasis—and, yes, even war. "Wars," a Georgist will say, "are always fought over land"—and we have the solution to the land problem, so... There you are.

Yet, when faced with yet another war, our enduring truths start to sound hollow, or even irrelevant. There's got to be something we can do, now! We yearn for some tangible thing we can accomplish toward stopping the violence and sharing our world in peace. We think, "Forget about the Law of Rent—We've got to stop the war!"

But what does it mean to stop a war? What is war, anyway? Our usual mental picture of "war" is really a large and an (oddly) comforting oversimplification.

Once the tanks are in the street or the planes are in the air, things are already way, far out of whack. When we say that a country is "at war," what we mean, unfortunately, is that its endemic state of violence and injustice has become whipped into such a frenzy that actual battle can no longer be put off.

If we steel ourselves and pursue this disconcerting line of thought, we come to realize that the difference between an army and a mob, or between a soldier and a terrorist, is much smaller than we had thought. The army is better-equipped than the mob. The terrorist usually provides his own clothing, and so is harder to spot in a crowd than the soldier.

I have no idea how there could truly be such a thing as an "honorable war"—or its evil reflection, a "war criminal." For if, let's say, we believe our nation's cause to be just and our enemy to be on the side of evil, then is it not our job to win, by any means necessary? Who are the war criminals? War is always criminal.

But, now—some would argue—what about a soldier who brutally and summarily mows down innocent civilians, is that not a war criminal? Well, where is the line? Innocent civilians are always killed in war—just as innocent civilians are always killed in conditions of abject poverty during what we normally call "times of peace." With a small fraction of its annual military expenditure, the United States could eliminate deaths from cholera and dysentery worldwide, by providing safe water supplies. If the people of the US choose instead to build advanced fighter planes, are they war criminals?

There is much more to war than battle, and there is certainly much more to peace than simply trying to stop the pitched fighting. If we can save people's lives by marching in demonstrations, or sitting in front of the tanks, then of course we must do those things. It's always a good thing to stop war. But: if we stop this war, will there be peace?

Not hardly. Peace is not just the absence of overt war. If we stop whatever shooting adventure happens to be going on, there will still be all the injustice, poverty, hatred, hopelessness—and still all the callous overindulgence. War is big news—but violence goes deep.

"If you want peace, work for justice." That's an old movement saw that is just as true as it ever was, and yet—I suspect that many of the people who have rallied around that call have been, nevertheless, in their heart of hearts, unclear about what justice actually entails. Surely Georgists have a contribution to make in that area, one that could go far toward truly building peace. We recognize that justice is not simply a matter of Robin-hooding and welfare; it is about the moral basis of ownership. Justice is about every human being's right to live and work on the earth, and to keep the fruits of one's own labor.

Our most important work is to teach justice. Sometimes it's appropriate, to be sure, to discuss a groovy way of invigorating cities by shifting the property tax. But we must also develop a vision. We must be able to articulate a clear, vibrant conception of what justice is and how it actually works. We must spread that message as quickly and efficiently as we possibly can; we must say it, not just over and over again because we're in the habit, but with passion.

And, of course, one is tempted to ask, "Is that enough?" But that isn't the relevant question, is it?—it's really, "What else will work?" If one person to whom you have spread the message goes out and faithfully spreads it to others, then you have accomplished work to build peace. That's how it's done; there's no shortcut.

~ *Georgist Journal* #96
September 2002

Wars become possible when lots of people on both sides persuade themselves to believe what their common-sense tells them is false: that it is worth sustaining infinite inconvenience and danger oneself; and inflicting infinite suffering on others, in order to sustain some vaguely-stated objective—political, religious or economic—which not one man in a thousand can explain.

~ *Roy Douglas*

— Chapter 4 —

Electoral Reform

Henry George believed that no revolution was necessary to bring about the First Great Reform he advocated; that the essential structures were already in place in modern society and existing laws need only be modified to secure private and public property on a moral basis. Perhaps in earnest of this (although the reason he cited for his first race was "to raise hell"), George accepted twice the challenge to run for Mayor of New York City. In 1886, George said he would run only if the United Labor Parties gathered 30,000 signatures requesting it—which they did. During George's life and the two decades following, the single tax movement was organized politically in the US and fielded many candidates. Notable single taxers in public office included Henry George, Jr., elected to the US Congress, Tom L. Johnson, Mayor of Cleveland, and Louis F. Post, Assistant Secretary of Labor in the administration of Woodrow Wilson. George was not naïve, however, about the corruption of the political system. In Social Problems, he states that "It behooves us to look facts in the face. The experiment of popular government in the United States in clearly a failure...our government by the people has become...government by the strong and unscrupulous."

Georgists realized that to achieve their great goals, it would be necessary not only to educate the people, but to ensure that the political system would faithfully carry out the people's wishes. Many got involved campaigns for electoral reform. One notable example was a successful effort in Oregon, spearheaded by single taxers, to initiate popular legislation by referendum. Many states have since adopted this reform. (Results have been mixed, however—as exemplified by California's notorious Proposition 13.)

There is a growing consensus that the US political system must be reformed. Voter turnout has been consistently dropping and polls show increasing anger and cynicism toward elected officials, particularly in the Congress. The two major parties offer less and less choice; they are widely perceived as differing mainly in their rhetorical stances. "Winner-take-all" campaigns between major-party candidates often use the ugly but effective technique of "mudslinging" rather than offering positive proposals. Many calls have been made for a reform of campaign finance. Campaign contributions by individuals have been limited by law since the 80s. However, a huge loophole was left open—individuals and corporations can legally give unlimited amounts to political parties (who then turn around and spend it on enormously expensive TV-intensive modern campaigns). Legislation to disallow this kind of "soft money," overwhelmingly supported by the public, have left loopholes big enough to render them ineffective.

Another poorly-understood process in US government that preserves the status quo is the use of redistricting to give a nearly irresistible demographic advantage to incumbents in Congressional and Senate races. Because this process is controlled by the very politicians who stand to benefit from it, there is a huge incentive to "gerrymander" districts. (The tactic of "gerrymandering"—redrawing districts to weaken opposition blocs—has long been controversial. After the Civil War it was used to weaken support for African-American legislators. More recently an "affirmative-action" form of gerrymandering was used to redress racial and ethnic imbalances.)

There is growing advocacy of a shift to a "proportional representation" system. Under such a system, voters rank the candidates, and legislators are elected according to a tally of their preference levels with voters. Under such a system, alternative political parties have a much better chance of influencing the legislative process. Voters no longer feel the need to "throw away" their votes on the lesser of two evils. Many nations use such a system today, including Germany, Japan, Australia and Brazil.

Some advocate using the new technological possibilities of instant communication to institute "direct democracy"—in other words, to bypass the representative system and, essentially, decide every legislative question by electronic referendum. Others point out, though, that well-financed modern advertisers can sway popular opinion virtually instantly. In an age of instant communication, when most of the content of that communication is in the control of huge media conglomerates, a fair and uncorrupt system of "direct electronic democracy" is hard to imagine.

Henry George believed that "democratic government in more than name can exist only where wealth is distributed with something like equality—where the great mass of citizens are personally free and independent, neither fettered by their poverty nor made subject by their wealth." And yet he proposed to use that very democratic system to bring about the reform that would create such a state of society. This could, perhaps, be called a paradox—or, a dual challenge to George's followers.

~ Adapted from HGI's, course in Applied Economics
~ Georgist Journal #100
Spring 2004

— Chapter 5 —

Why Are Theories of Value Important?

The idea of value was an important topic in the development of political economy, yet modern-day economics has little to say about it. For example, *Economics* by Samuelson and Nordhaus, does not trouble to define "value" at all—doesn't even mention it in its index. On the other hand, the concept of "price" is extensively explored. This represents the shift from a "normative" science of political economy, which seeks to design and build a just society, to a "positive" study of economics, which seeks to analyze facts and behavior, avoiding the notions of "ought" and "should."

> You call me a socialist. I suppose you'll have to admit that I'm rather a peculiar one! I have been a Georgist for more than 50 years. I support a completely free price-mechanism controlled market. I am a free trader and would like nothing better than to have the US drop all tariffs, quotas, anti-dumping duties the first thing tomorrow morning. I want minimum government and an end to privilege. Privilege to a Georgist is "privilege" or private law. That is, a law designed to take from one to give to another. This major Georgist theme—the ending of privilege—unites people across the political spectrum. Privilege is the opposite of justice and the phrase "liberty and justice for all" requires the ending of privilege.
>
> *~ Harry Pollard*
> *on the "Land Theory" email list*

However, very few people are content with the present state of the "body economic." All manner of "oughts" and "shoulds" are constantly being proposed. It seems that we are not yet through with the notion of value.

The major debate about value has always been about whether it inherent in things, or is a function of human desires. Plato regarded value as inherent in a commodity, but Aristotle attributed it to a commodity's utility, and he said the standard of value lies in wants. Thus the field was divided, for ever more, between the "left" and the "right."

The Labor Theory

The "labor theory of value"—the idea that the value of a thing is a function of the labor expended in creating it—was a tenet of the classical economists, especially David Ricardo. Its influence today, however, is mainly due to Karl Marx. According to Marx, the value of a commodity tends to be the "amount of labor time socially necessary" to produce it. This is most clearly seen in the mode of production called capitalism, under which commodities are produced, by unskilled laborers, for sale in the market. The laborers exchange their labor time for wages, and the "capitalists" own both the means of production and the products.

What does "socially necessary" mean? It is defined as the amount of labor required to produce a thing under the normal conditions of production at a given time. In the capitalist mode of production, the "labor value" of a thing is made up of three parts: Constant capital (the equipment and location needed) Variable capital (the workers' wages) and Surplus value (the parasitical "cut" taken by the Capitalist class). All of the items in turn that go into the category of Constant capital (commodities themselves, such as a truck, a printing press or a factory) likewise have a labor value composed of these three elements.

Under capitalism, there exists at any given time a general rate of profit—which is simply an average of all the rates of profit in the various micro-markets. If the rate of profit for a certain commodity equals the general rate of profit, then the surplus value of that commodity equals its profit to the capitalist, and its market price tends to equal its labor value. Of course, some commodities bring higher—or lower-than-average profits. In such cases, the commodity's labor value will not match its "price of production"—and comparing the two will be helpful to the economic planner (who will, eventually, have to determine optimum production levels, without the helpful feedback of prices).

According to Marxist analysis, capitalists invest in production in order to collect surplus value. However, competition for market share will put a downward pressure on profits. Capitalists will have to reduce wages (which will, in turn, reduce demand for commodities, leading to "overproduction" and depressions). The deterioration of conditions for workers will inflames class antagonism and lead to revolution. Then, the workers themselves, coming together to seize the means of production, will use the efficiency of modern industrial production for their own benefit.

The division of "labor value" into its three components gives us a glimpse of how a socialist economy could ever hope to achieve efficient resource allocation. Surplus value is, supposedly, the value of exploitation in a capitalist society, over and above the costs of Labor (Variable capital), and Land + Capital (Constant capital). If—according to Marxist theory—this exploitative surcharge were not imposed on the cost of every commodity produced, there would be a vast fund available for raising wages, providing social services, and "scientifically planning" an efficient socialist economy.

However, under the capitalist mode of production, decisions about "what?" "how many?" and "for whom?" are made with the invaluable aid of the invisible hand of a (more or less) free market. The market, though, is precisely what leads to surplus value and (to Marxists) all the structural failings of capitalism. Under the next phase of history—socialism—allocation decisions would not be made by the "higgling of the market," but by some form of objective planning. This is where the labor theory of value comes in very handy.

If value is not inherent in the commodity, but is a subjective determination of the buyer(s), then socialist "scientific planning" has no basis. For a planned economy to be workable at all, value must be inherent in things. If the amount of labor embodied in a thing is a quantity that can be observed and measured, then it becomes possible for "scientific planning" to achieve efficient production patterns.

Marxist theory, then, utterly depends on an objective theory of value.

The Subjective Theory

The other major contender for a modern theory of value is the Austrian theory, which traces its roots to Principles of Economics by Carl Menger. It tells us that value is subjective. It has nothing to do with anything inherent in a commodity, including the amount of labor that went into it. It is simply a matter of how much each individual wants each thing.

To Austrian economists, if a glass of water is sold for a million dollars to someone who is dying of thirst, then, by golly, that's its value. A more conventional view would hold that, because of special circumstances, the glass was sold for more than its market value. But Austrian theory holds that there is no such thing as the "market value" of a good; value is revealed in particular transactions. One could compute an average of the various observed prices for which a good has sold, but that can only lead to an approximation of the thing's value.

Why is that important? Because if there is such a thing as "market value," then it becomes possible for things to be sold for more than their market value—in other words, it becomes possible for markets to fail. Monopoly, or subsidy, or political manipulation, might end up allowing sellers to pocket the gleanings of "market failure," enriching themselves at the expense of the community. This, then, would lead to various kinds of interventions in the free market, to remove the unfairness of "market failures." (To Marxists, remember, failure is inherent in the market economy.)

In order to correct supposed imperfections in the market allowing some "monopolists" to capitalize on "market failure," government imposes restrictions on free-market behavior! In Austrian theory, this represents the very worst kind of circular reasoning. (Free-market economists tend to believe that monopolies, far from being parasitical, benefit society by affording innovators the extra capital they need to create the means for industrial progress.)

If "market failure" exists at all, Austrian economists see it as a conflict between individuals or groups in their plans to use certain scarce resources. Efficient resolutions to these conflicts can be negotiated between the interested parties—but not if the resources are removed from the market process by confiscation or regulation.

This gets us back to the question of why value theory is important: If the value of a commodity is inherent, then it is possible for it to have a "true" value that is different from what it exchanges for in a particular transaction. This would open the door to intervention—to the temptation to remove things from that free interplay of individual desires, and individual plans for satisfying them, that constitute economic activity.

If the value of things is only revealed in free individual transactions, then the community should never—and has no right to—interfere in those transactions. If anything that could be held privately is, instead, held communally by the coercive power of the state, then the free interplay of desires and plans is restricted; economic activity and freedom are retarded.

Austrian theory holds that ethical concerns have no place in economic theory. Society might decide, out of some over-arching social concern, to communalize certain assets—but in doing so it would always limit human freedom. In the Austrian view of things, there is an inevitable trade-off between government intervention and the just, efficient society in which individual freedom is maximized.

The Problem with Land

It's interesting to note that each of these "competing" theories of value encounters a pretty serious stumbling block when it comes to the question of land. Marxist theory accounts for the value of land as part of the "Constant capital" that goes into the production of commodities. Land itself isn't produced by labor, of course—so it can only acquire value when labor is applied to it in some way. This is reminiscent of J. S. Mill's justification for property in land, which Henry George critiques in *The Science of Political Economy*. Land can become private property, according to Mill, when (and because) it is improved. Under the Labor Theory, that is also why it acquires value. However, it is evident that unimproved land can indeed have value—for we see huge amounts of value tied up in urban locations that stand completely idle, with no labor applied to them at all, sometimes for decades.

Austrian theorists also get caught in a vicious circle when it comes to land. This is not because land value is not subjective, measuring the land's utility to the buyer; indeed it is. However, Austrian theory holds that unrestricted privatization leads to efficient allocation and promotes human freedom. This certainly seems to be true in the case of the products of labor—but it is clearly untrue in the case of land. Although some still try to justify it, using exotic interpretations of allocative efficiency, the evidence is overwhelming that private collection of land rent leads to economic dysfunction. (Public collection of the legitimate products of labor and capital does, too—but free-market theorists are eager to agree with that.)

George's Great Reconciliation

One of Henry George's most powerful attributes as a social philosopher is his unswerving faith that social science, if it is correctly based on natural law, cannot lead society to violence or decay. On the one hand, we have a Labor Theory of Value. Reasoning logically therefrom, we determine that justice can only be secured by removing the great vitality that society gains from the free market. On the other hand, we have a Subjective Theory of Value, which leads us to a "best of all possible worlds" in which our access to the natural opportunities, which all of us need to sustain life, must be purchased from private owners, for the sake of "freedom"!

George examined the theory that value depends on the labor embodied in a thing, and found it absurd; simple observation showed that value is not inherent, but a function of the buyers' desires. However, simple observation also demonstrated that private ownership of everything—whether or not it is a product of human labor—leads neither to justice nor efficiency. He managed cut through this dilemma by introducing the concept of "value from obligation." George saw that the amount of value is subjective—determined by nothing more than the "higgling of the market." However, the source of value is not subjective! It depends on one all-important objective quality of a thing: whether it was or was not produced by human labor.

This distinction means nothing to the individual; land, stocks, money or physical wealth all have the same kind of value to us, as individuals. A political economy that sees the aggregate as nothing more than the sum of all individual transactions would, likewise, see no importance in the distinction between value from production and value from obligation. But George's analysis shows us that there exists a subset of value that cannot be attributed to individual inputs, but to the activity of the entire community.

So: labor is not the source of all value—but it is the source of some value: the value that comes from production—and, the amount of value a commodity has is subjective, bearing no relation whatever to that value's source. With this firm theoretical foundation, George could confidently build an economic theory that could reconcile freedom and justice, proving his contention that "justice is the highest and truest expediency."

This essay is part of the reading for the HGIs course in Economic Science.
~ *Georgist Journal* #104
April, 2006

— Chapter 6 —

Political Economy and Services

Georgists set great store in Henry George's scheme of economic definitions—and rightly so; they are a powerful logical tool. "Once you understand these definitions," I have told students, "you can actually infer the whole rest of the course." The ability to unambiguously divide the economic world into three mutually-exclusive factors makes everything easier, especially when compared to the trackless wastes of conventional, neoclassical theory. Political economy, Henry George tells us, is "the science which treats of the nature of wealth and the laws of its production and distribution."

George's neat scheme of definitions runs into a bit of a snag over the question of services. In George's view, services—defined as valuable processes resulting in not the creation of material goods, but rather the direct satisfaction of desire—are not the main thing. In *The Science of Political Economy* he puts it this way:

> *The barber, the singer, the physician, and the actor do not produce wealth, but direct satisfactions. But not only are their efforts which are expended in this way mainly devoted to the procurement of wealth, which they get in exchange for their services, but any exchange between themselves of services for services takes place through the medium of wealth. To this we may add that the laws which govern the production and distribution of services are essentially the same as those which govern the production and distribution of wealth. Thus we see that all the ends of political economy may be reached if its inquiry be an inquiry into the nature of wealth and the laws that govern its production and distribution.*

George's reasoning, usually crystal-clear, is a tad murky here. It is entirely possible for people to exchange services for services without any mediation of wealth. And if the laws that govern the production and distribution of services are essentially the same as those that deal with wealth, then why the distinction?

Furthermore, George clearly understands that the point of economic activity (despite his stated definition) is not to provide people with valuable stuff (wealth), but rather to satisfy their desires.

> ...*wealth is not the only result of human exertion, nor is it indeed the final cause of human exertion. That is not reached until wealth is spent or consumed in satisfaction of desire. Wealth itself is in fact only a halting-place or storehouse on the way between prompting desire and final satisfaction; a point at which exertion, journeying towards the satisfaction of desire, remains for a time stored up in concrete form, and from whence it may be called forth to yield the satisfaction which is its ultimate aim. And there are exertions aiming at the satisfaction of desire which do not pass through the form of wealth at all.*

The "barber, the singer, the physician and the actor" exert labor in the production of services, and they are paid for this. It would seem, then, that what they do is part of political economy, and that they get a portion of the "wages" slice of the overall wealth pie. Seems straightforward enough. But, along comes a literal reader of George to point out that, by definition, "the wealth pie" includes wealth only, not services—and therefore, wages paid to services are some sort of secondary distribution of wealth, perhaps akin to taxation, or theft, in that the return to services is "not part of political economy." And, well, I guess one could put it that way, but I have no idea what would be clarified or explained by doing so. For one thing, services are quite unlike theft (or taxation of production, which is morally theft). Services are freely undertaken and compensated at their market value. Furthermore, although we tend to think of labor providing services, there are many ways in which the other factors also provide the direct satisfaction of desires. A public restroom, for example, is capital that provides a service. As with all capital there is labor involved in its maintenance—but the capital itself is what satisfies our desires there. And, in terms of land:

people will pay admission fees just to gaze upon a distinctive natural vista—the Grand Canyon, say. Our desire is to see the beautiful place, and the Grand Canyon satisfies it directly. Egad! This means that some services aren't even produced by labor!

One might ask why this discussion is important for anyone but a couple of crusty old Georgists debating theory in the library of the Henry George School, far from light or relevance. I would suggest, though, that the 19th-century attitude embodied in "why political economy considers only wealth" is a large—but entirely removable—stumbling block in the way of modern application of George's thought. George set out to understand and remedy the processes by which rapid material advances in production brought poverty and industrial depression in their wake. These processes had everything to do with the production of material wealth. George had no inclination to consider any downsides or limits to the amazing march of improvement in the arts of production. He was bullish on population, quipping that "the earth could maintain a thousand billions of people as easily as a thousand millions." Elsewhere, of course, he qualified that rather nonsensical statement by affirming that the solution to the problem mistakenly called "overpopulation" is the natural demographic shift that comes with a certain level of human progress. Nevertheless, like other writers of his day, Henry George didn't think in terms of "carrying capacity" or any potential for "global environmental catastrophes." Nowadays we do, though.

What has all this to do with the role of services in political economy? Quite a lot. The ultimate aim of political economy, George tells us, is the satisfaction of desires. Writing as he did in a time of flourishing industrial progress, he could perhaps be excused for seeing that as a moot point. Services are well and good; but they aren't very important; they follow the same laws as wealth, and wealth is the main thing. However, the 21st Century has brought us a new class of desires that cannot be satisfied with stuff. It's fashionable in some circles today to talk of "ecosystem services"—such as the capacity of the earth's atmosphere to soak up the waste gases of our incessant industry and transportation. That's a bona fide service, provided by the natural world, that's getting more valuable all the time. Political economy really can't avoid considering such things.

Henry George's instincts were right on the money, even if his frame of reference made it difficult for him to see the implications. At a certain stage of civilization, the production of wealth is everything: providing food, clothing and shelter is, by far, the most important aspect of economic activity. But as material progress advances, higher-order desires for luxury, artistic or scientific things gain more importance. The consumption of services—haircuts, national parks, internet cafes—is part of this process. Eventually there comes a day when our desire for less—less pollution and environmental degradation—starts to take on great prominence.

George's insistence that "political economy only consider wealth" seems to suggest that he would regard the GDP as a more-or-less acceptable indicator of economic progress. Many Georgist sympathizers today, however, most emphatically do not. Unfortunately, however, attempts to fashion a more complete or responsible indicator often make the mistake of incorporating subjective elements that make a mockery of rational economic analysis. Henry George did not fall into that trap. He neatly cut the normative/positive knot, by challenging society to remove privilege, and then let the market be free.

George was on the right track in saying that the basic point of economic activity is the satisfaction of human desires. In the twenty-first century, one profoundly important desire is that the human experiment on earth find a way to sustain itself without destroying its home. Were he writing today, George would have no trouble connecting the dots. He'd define political economy as: "the science which treats of the nature of economic value, and the laws governing the production and distribution of valuable goods and services." It doesn't roll as neatly off the tongue, but neither does it torture logic.

~ *Georgist Journal* #109
April 2008

— Chapter 7 —

Are We Disreputable?

Should we be concentrating on the B region, or the A region, of that glass of water? Ah, well—psychologically, motivationally, we know the answer, but at times it's a little hard to keep the faith. Recently I've gotten three rather telling signals of how much traction Georgism, or the Single Tax, is getting in today's marketplace of ideas, and the news isn't good.

First we have "the new Schalkenbach film," which is discussed herein by Richard Giles, and which we will have an opportunity to see at the upcoming CGO conference in Kansas City. We have heard that Henry George's Remedy (by that or any other name) will not be mentioned in the film. The reason for that is more practical than perfidious. The filmmaker, Philippe Diaz, is an accomplished, award-winning professional, who knows that moviegoers have no interest in being educated about political economy. He is fashioning a potential hit in the burgeoning "Ain't It Awful" market.

Last year, Frances Moore Lappé published a (useful, worthwhile) book titled *Getting a Grip: Clarity, Creativity, and Courage in a World Gone Mad*. In it she made frequent mention of Lizzie Magie Phillips, the original inventor, as we know, of Monopoly (*aka* The Landlord's Game). Lizzie's work is extolled as an example of a creative contribution to making things better by crafting a popular, accessible way to teach people about economic injustice. All true and good—except that Lappé did not see fit to mention, anywhere (not even in a footnote) what ideas Magie sought to teach in her game!

Then we have John Médaille, an author who, like Lappé, is well worth reading, with many good and thoughtful things to say. Yet in response to my review, which took him to task for seeming to write as though Henry George's books had never actually existed, he bluntly replies:

I know well that texts with too much of George are regarded as Georgist texts, and placed in the Georgist file, a round file which most publishers keep near their desks. I was not, at this stage, willing to fight that battle...

Does it not seem, friends, that Georgists, Single Taxers, Rent-as-Revenue Freaks, are a bit—shall we say—disreputable? What do you suppose ought to be done about this?

We seem to have two options. On the one hand, we could be well-behaved. We could accept the fact of suburban sprawl and analyze of its social ramifications. When we're feeling especially brave, we could mention that the property tax might not actually be so bad. We'll carefully examine what various groups want to hear, and craft a series of supportive messages. Most important, we'll never, ever, utter the name "Henry George" or betray any fellow-traveling with "normative economics."

Or? We could embrace our dangerous, smoking-under-the-bleachers status; we could be rebels with a cause. Every rebellious notion isn't, after all, automatically wrong. We could look our critics in the eye—with a slouch and a sneer, maybe, why not?—and say, "Yeah, there is a moral basis of ownership. The rent of land does belong to the community. You wanna make something of it?"

It's not like we have so terribly much to lose. We have *The American Journal of Economics and Sociology*, and a handful of tenured professors. That's about as much mainstream respectability as we're likely to get anytime soon. Meanwhile, people in US prisons, and people on the street in places like Nicaragua, Nigeria, Ghana and India, get excited about what we have to say. Georgism is disreputable? Cool!

~ *Georgist Journal* #109
April 2008

— Chapter 8 —

A Georgist Stand on Corporate Privilege?

Georgists are sometimes accused of having taken rather too direct a path back from the heights of inspiration. Sophisticated friends warn that "things just aren't that simple." Now, I, for one, am not dismayed by this. I really like Henry George's contention that once we implement his simple philosophy, we'll then be free to give adequate attention to all the things in heaven and earth that it dreams not of.

But we're often admonished that the timeless principles of Georgism need updating. Such advice frequently comes from "guns for hire" who want to use Georgists' money to save them from their lack of vision. The poor Georgists have been purveying this land thing for so long, with such little success; they just don't know any better, poor lambs. Such "miserable comforters" should be chucked whence they came—but frustrated advocates, with precious little by way of real success to build on, are easily tempted. And thus, the very real question of updating and modernizing the Georgist message is complicated and—dare I say—sometimes subverted.

One area into which we often feel a need to weigh is that of the vast, increasing power of corporations. They surely seem to be exploiting some sort of privilege, and shouldn't we, as purveyors of fundamental economic justice, say something about that? I mean, can it really all be about land? Agnes George deMille seemed to be heading in this direction in her stirring words on the centenary of *Progress and Poverty*:

The great sinister fact, the one that we must live with, is that we are yielding up sovereignty. The nation is no longer comprised of the thirteen original states, nor of the thirty-seven younger sister states, but of the real powers: the cartels, the corporations. Owning the bulk of our productive resources, they are the issue of that concentration of ownership that George saw evolving, and warned against. These multinationals are not American any more. Transcending nations, they serve not their country's interests, but their own. They manipulate our tax policies to help themselves. They determine our statecraft. They are autonomous. They do not need to coin money or raise armies. They use ours.

True enough. So what is to be done, about this "great sinister fact"?

A corporation is an entity recognized in law as an "artificial person" possessing rights enjoyed by real persons, such as freedom of speech (which frequently takes the form of campaign contributions) and due process of law. Corporations in the United States come into being when they are chartered, which happens at the state level, and unlike actual persons they exist forever, unless something extraordinary happens such as bankruptcy, or revocation of their charter. The great advantage of the corporate form of business organization is that a corporation can raise large sums of money by issuing stock. The shareholders, who collectively own the corporation, share in the profits via dividends, and/or bet that their shares will increase in value. However, the corporation's liability for any illegal or harmful action is limited to the assets of the corporation itself—not those of the shareholders. The most that they can lose is the value of the shares they hold. We could view this in a positive sense as providing the means to create large, progressive, risky and expensive endeavors, the kind that move forward a great nation's economy—but we could also leaven our enthusiasm with Ambrose Bierce's definition of a corporation as "an ingenious device for obtaining individual profit without individual responsibility."

A seminal Georgist document on this issue was the lecture by John Z. White on the Dartmouth College Decision, which appeared in *The St. Louis Mirror*, and later in *The Public*, in 1906. The *Dartmouth College Decision* was the US Supreme Court decision, written by Chief Justice John Marshall in 1819, which held that the state of New Hampshire could not revoke the charter of Dartmouth College, because it was a legal contract between the college and the English Sovereign which, containing no provision for dissolution, could not be revoked by the state without unconstitutionally breaking a contract. White found this patently absurd. His essay skillfully illuminates every facet of a point that is in fact, by its essential nature, quite obvious. That point is that a corporate charter is not a contract, despite all manner of eloquent statements that it is; it is a grant of privilege which the state, having the sovereign power to grant, can remove. White notes that the doctrine of a corporation as a legal person is embedded in this mistaken decision—because in order for there to be a contract, there must be some person with whom the contract was made. Thus, according to the decision, an infinitesimal instant transpired between the creation of the legal person named Dartmouth College, and the sealing of a contract with that, uhm, person.

John Z. White had recourse to a Single Taxer's clarity as regards public and private property. This is a tremendous advantage when discussing thorny matters of law. It's a strategy that could actually get some traction in the mainstream press in 1906—but, alas, today, not so much. He quotes Marshall: "A grant of corporate powers and privileges is as much a contract as a grant of land." White goes on to hoist Marshall by his own petard, in another decision referring to a land grant:

> *This grant is a contract, the object of which is, that the profits issuing from it shall inhere to the benefit of the grantee... Yet the power of taxation may be carried so far as to absorb these profits. Does this impair the obligation of contracts? The idea is rejected by all...*

In short, for White the Dartmouth College decision used a legal technicality to establish a precedent of inviolability for corporate charters. The legal status of corporations was further strengthened by the 1886 decision in *Santa Clara County vs. Southern Pacific Railroad*, in which corporations were held to have the rights of persons, as guaranteed in the Bill of Rights, and the 14th Amendment's Equal Protection clause.

But just how harmful is all this? If corporations do indeed have too much power and too little accountability (as seems only too evident), what is to be done about it? These are, I think, fair questions. We're Georgists, and we ought to work to our strengths: less chanting "Ain't It Awful"; more fundamental solutions.

It's worth noting that John Z. White was writing before either the individual or the corporate income tax, before a host of federal regulations protecting worker and consumer safety, and the environment, and at a very early stage of the organized labor movement. All of these things seemed—for a while anyway—effective ways to enforce a certain level of corporate responsibility. Yet, today, corporations seem to be striking back with great power, and pretty much having their own way of things. The "race to the bottom" seems to be entirely for the corporations' benefit. So what must be done? Should corporate charters be revoked? Should corporations be socked with much higher taxes? Should shareholders be compelled to insure themselves against corporate malfeasance? Or—do corporations simply make use of the potential efficiencies granted to them, in order to consolidate deeper levels of privilege and maldistribution?

Georgists are somewhat divided on the issue. Jeff Smith has consistently espoused his "geonomic" position that:

> The corporate charter's salient feature is to limit the liability of those choosing to profit by putting others at risk.... Charters, and their companion pieces of legislation, are worth to those corporations putting nature, labor, and consumer at risk however much that year insurance companies would charge them, i.e., the losses due to unsafe products, workplaces, and pollution and depletion—hundreds of billions annually.[1]

Meanwhile, Fred Foldvary has consistently countered that:

The real privilege is not the corporation as an institution, but from the privileges granted to enterprise in general. Companies world-wide are granted subsidies to destroy and use up natural resources, such as roads in forests paid for by government and dams financed by the World Bank. They are allowed to pollute, with taxpayers financing dysfunctional regulations. Much of their profit can consist of the rent of land that they did not create, and whose value derives from government services they do not pay for. Workers get low wages and suffer poor working conditions because their governments block off alternative opportunities and confiscate much of their meager gains with taxes on incomes, sales, and wealth. Harmful products are sold by fraud, with no consumer warnings or notices to buyers who mistakenly think government protects them.[2]

Despite what seems, at first glance, to be a substantial impasse, I imagine that both commentators would agree with the following observation by Henry George, Jr., a year before John Z. White's speech:

If... the privilege of land monopoly be destroyed by the process of taxation, if the privilege of highway monopoly be transferred to public hands, if tariff and other taxation privileges be wiped out, what important privilege would remain for exploitation through incorporation? The only possible use to which an artificial person, or corporation, could be put would be that of engaging in the production of wealth where there was an open and free field, where no one had any favor. What matter then if a corporation be organized "infinite in scope, perpetual in character, vested in the hands of a few, with methods secret even to stockholders"?[3]

Nevertheless: this is where Georgists tend to get into trouble. It starts to seem that every time someone brings up a problem: AIDS in Africa, desertification, urban blight, poor-quality TV programs, inexplicable pop songs, the heartbreak of psoriasis—Georgists say everything would be fine, everything would be fine—if only we'd tax land values and bring the margin back. OK, I admit it; it makes us sound a bit Wack.

But the problem is, it's... kind of... true. If rational analysis showed these other issues to be as important as the fundamental laws of distribution, and moral basis of ownership, then Georgists would deserve the accusations of fetishizing a 19th-century panacea at the cost of losing all hope for effectiveness. But the Law of Rent is unrepealable; we've just got to deal with that. And very, very few people understand what we mean by that. We've got to deal with that, too—either that or just stay drunk all the time.

Debate will go on about whether the corporate charter is, in itself, dangerously unjust and harmful. Debate will go on, in a similar vein, over money and banking, international trade, immigration, global warming and a host of other topical issues. These are all important and subtle topics; lots of smart people write reams of provocative copy about them. We Georgists, I think, do well to become sufficiently familiar with these issues as to be able to discuss them without drooling. But we should keep our eyes on the prize. Our sights are on "the robber that takes all that is left." Very few people have as clear a view of that robber as we do. We're not going to clarify other people's vision by blurring our own.

~ *Georgist Journal* #109
April 2008

End Notes

1. http://www.progress.org/archive/subsidy01.htm

2. http://www.progress.org/archive/fold198.htm

3. http://www.progress.org/archive/hgjr25c.htm

— Chapter 9 —

Does Georgism Have a Theory of History?

The time is always now for Georgists. It's one of our most endearing quirks—or most annoying eccentricities, as the case may be. We tout a proposal for correcting fundamental economic wrongs—diseases that afflict any system in any time in which The Remedy has not been applied. Take a quick skim of the Georgist press in any period between the 1880s and today. You'll see that *this* was the time, that *today's* problems would propel society to finally wise up and look to real solutions.

It has been suggested that Georgism, to the extent that is has evolved—or seeks to evolve—beyond a quick-fix-it plan into a system of thought, lacks a theory of history and would do well to devise one. We might see a symptom of this in the persistence of Georgist educators (including, unabashedly, the *Henry George Institute*) in asking students to read the works of Henry George himself. We could be accused, I suppose, of hanging slavishly on Henry George's every word. Could George's writings really be that timeless? Did the man get every single thing right?

Which is not to say he didn't get most of it, right on the money. The observation that land's rental value rises as a community's population, sophistication and interconnectedness—and therefore its need for public revenue—grows. The notion that a thing's value can come from two sources, production or obligation. The insight that a communal feeling—the desire for approbation—trumps mere selfishness as a core motivation. The point that society progresses to the extent that it fosters equality and association, and declines to the extent that it thwarts those things. The challenge of the increasing importance of social questions as society becomes more interconnected. Those are a few of my favorites; I'm sure you can think of more.

Our world-changing comrades, the Marxists, have a very strong—one might almost say overbearing—theory of history that leads directly to their version of the Good Society. The logic of historical materialism invests Marxist rhetoric with great confidence, and gives Marxist academics plenty to write about. Drastically simplified, this theory holds that class struggle is inherent in capitalism and intensifies with every social and/or technological increase in worker productivity. Eventually this makes the lives of industrial workers, the proletariat, intolerable. They will then dare to seize control of the means of production and create a socialist state. Once the capitalist class has been divested of its means of controlling the masses, the state will wither away, leaving a stateless, classless society. This, from a Marxist point of view, is what will happen; the only argument is exactly where "now" is to be placed on the dialectical timeline.

Folks on the left, hearing about the Georgist remedy, ask, "So, do you believe that can happen without a revolution?" And I have to admit that not only am I not sure, but more importantly that my answer to that question comes from my own predilections, independent of and, probably, prior to anything I've learned about Georgist philosophy. Where does Georgism stand on the question of class struggle?

Henry George recognized the existence of such a thing. The effects of material progress were, he wrote, "as though an immense wedge were being forced, not underneath society, but through society. Those who are above the point of separation are elevated, but those who are below are crushed down." Yet George couldn't point to a clearly-defined group of villains to blame for all this. He took pains to show that it wasn't capital; defined as mere physical wealth, a product of labor, capital couldn't possibly be the exploiter of labor. On the other hand, capital defined as the means by which one group exploits the labor of another group, well—that wasn't what George was talking about; that definition was too vague to be useful to him. And the landowner wasn't really the bad guy either:

there are lots of small, hardworking landowners who stand to gain a net benefit under George's remedy. Who, then, would be the people who would struggle—against which other people—to bring the Georgist Good Society into being? George dedicated *Progress and Poverty* to "…those who, seeing the vice and misery that spring from the unequal distribution of wealth and privilege, feel the possibility of a higher social state and would strive for its attainment." These would be the people who would take up "the cross of a new crusade"—a crusade that would offer deeper rewards than mere success.

Unlike Marx, George didn't see society as moving along a teleological arrow. George believed that human civilization would always come to a fork in the road, at which it could either ascend to the Good Society of equality and association, or decline into barbarism. Indeed, the rise and fall of civilizations, in George's view, can be seen as a long-run manifestation of the rise and fall of prosperity in boom-bust cycles. The same fundamental institution causes both; there's only one way to get off the roller coaster.

So did Henry George view history as merely cyclical? Not entirely; he did see civilization as moving in a direction. A civilization could be cast down and reset at its material beginning, but it would nevertheless move through certain stages as it rose. George saw society generally moving from local to international, and from self-reliant to interdependent. Particularly, he thought that a primitive state of production which was driven by skill would inevitably be superseded by a modern one in which knowledge took precedence. George was bullish on industrialization, which would allow—once the dead weights of rent and taxation were lifted from workers—for shorter and shorter workdays and wider and wider sharing of cultural amenities.

Social development is in accordance with certain immutable laws. And the law of development… is the law of integration. It is in obedience to this law—a law evidently as all-compelling as the law of gravitation—that these new agencies, which so powerfully stimulate social growth, tend to the specialization and interdependence of industry. It is in obedience to this law that the factory is superseding the independent mechanic, the large farm is swallowing up the little one, the big store shutting up the small one, that corporations are arising that dwarf the State, and that population tends more and more to concentrate in cities. Men must work together in larger and in more closely related groups. Production must be on a greater scale... Even butter and cheese are now made and chickens hatched and fattened in factories. (*The Land Question*)

Now this is a striking passage, and one that could be quoted rather damningly by today's progressive-minded folk. Henry George a supporter of Big-box retailers and factory chicken farms? Egad! It seems that the normally prescient George went rather off the rails on this point. But, before we revoke George's "green" card, we should remember that it's hard—probably impossible—for any writer to transcend his frame of reference. Industrial progress in his day was speedy, and accelerating. Socialists envisioned a technological workers' paradise in which labor hours would be short, varied, and demand no skills at all—a scenario with which Henry George seemed not to have a problem.

George did recognize, however, that sometimes the bigness of modern society represented not progress but distortion.

Trade as it is carried on today does involve much unnecessary transportation, and... producer and consumer are in many cases needlessly separated... Everywhere that modern civilization extends, and with greatest rapidity where its influences are most strongly felt, population and wealth are concentrating in huge towns and an exhausting commerce flows from country to city. But this ominous tendency is not natural, and does not arise from too much freedom; it is unnatural, and arises from restrictions. It may be clearly traced to monopolies, of which the monopoly of material opportunities is the first and most important. (*Protection or Free Trade*)

This "wasteful overtransportation of goods" is an integral part of the nasty syndrome that's currently referred to as "globalization." Goods made by subsistance-wage workers under unsafe conditions are shipped, using subsidized, atmosphere-destroying energy to be sold in corporate outlets that undersell local producers and destroy communities! Could such entrenched perniciousness really be addressed by something as simple, as cleanly theoretical as... The Single Tax?

Well, actually—yes, it could. There are a wagon-load of good reasons why, and as Georgist teachers, we should be careful not to get sidetracked on Henry George's evident—but small—mistakes. In this case, it seems clear to me that George didn't conceive of a state of society in which industrial development *per se* could be seen as regressive and damaging—in other words, a society that, even if it had the Single Tax, would see positive benefit in moving toward local production and away from centralization.

I think that's where we find ourselves today. Now it may be that the Single Tax, with its many ramifications, would ferret out, and gobble up, all the externalities that make corporate control and all its "wasteful over-transportation" profitable, which would make this whole point moot in the end. It's more likely, though, that the Single Tax would enable the kind of prosperity that would give people the luxury of time and resources to devote to their local environments, and to the inefficient, but oh-so-satisfying development of *skills*.

What is it, after all, that millions of us do when we get the chance to retire from the job market? We take up a hobby—which demands that we learn new skills, which we gladly do for pleasure, and to gird our brains against aging. Furthermore, though we tend to view it as romantic and impracticable, we admire those who are able to make a living by using a skill, rather than by applying some knowledge, acting like (and being replaceable by) just one more cog in a machine. Carpenters, painters, artisans of all kinds, hunters who actually know how to stalk game, cooks who know how to season dishes with the herbs they grow—we admire them, and when we can afford it, we pay premium prices for the products and services they offer. So, hey, maybe Henry George didn't actually foresee that we'd want to do such things. He did, however, posit that human beings seek to satisfy their desires—*whatever those desires are*—with the least exertion. No harm, no foul.

I suppose that this leaves us without a truly coherent theory of history with which to contest the Marxists. But I wonder how bad that really is. I'm reminded of George's contention, in the conclusion to *Progress and Poverty*, that "beyond the problem of social life lies the problem of individual life." It may be that beyond the problem of *economic* history—which is, after all, ultimately resolvable to the satisfaction of everyone—lies the problem of cultural history, which is multifarious, intimately complex, and beyond the comfortable bounds of theory. We're definitely not going to be able to get serious about that unless we can count on a just and prosperous economic order.

~ *Georgist Journal* #111
January 2009

— Chapter 10 —

A Georgist Theory of History: Work in Progress

One criticism frequently leveled at Georgists that has more truth than most is the notion that our analysis lacks depth—that we're shake 'n bake utopians, that we have one simple, magical cure to offer for poverty, depression, oppression, repression and indigestion. Henry George himself was, perhaps, guilty of creating that impression in the apocalyptic tone of many of his final chapters. Georgists fervently preach their One Great Law: "Tax land values and do as thou wilt…" At times, this makes our more sophisticated, credentialed colleagues a tad uneasy. I have seen the urgent *for-God's-sake-sit-down!* gestures at conference Q&A sessions. There's this nagging sense that we're just not quite up to speed, intellectually. This has sometimes led to a disavowal of certain terms, such as "Henry George," "Georgism," "Single Tax," "Rent," or even "Land"—as if uttering these words will reveal us as having come in with that discredited band of cranks.

Where such criticism is deserved—and it sometimes is—the problem can be addressed with a dose of good old-fashioned professionalism, and intellectual curiosity. Some of us could indeed do with a bit more "following truth where it leads" and a bit less self-referential insularity.

But I would like this criticism *not* to be deserved; I would like "being a Georgist" not to be something to be apologetic about. There are plenty of "Marxists" out there who proudly stand as such, despite perhaps not revering every word of *Das Kapital* as Revealed Truth; there are loads of "Keynesians" who may, or may not, place a "Neo" in front of the term. Good grief, even "Ricardians" publish papers from time to time—so why wouldn't we admit to being "Georgists"? If we're scholars, we'd better assert that George's position in intellectual history (not to mention his relevance to contemporary policy) doesn't depend on a popularity contest.

The Georgist movement has been, for the most part, more polemical than scholarly, and that is not necessarily a bad thing. Scholarship is as scholarship does, and unfortunately, much of today's "scholarly" work in economics amounts to self-serving, publish-or-perish journal-fodder. Not that some of it isn't interesting and insightful—but there's just so much of it to sift through. Both Neoclassical and Marxist economists have rich lodes of material for this sort of thing; the former have their mathematical models, while the latter have endlessly nuanced interpretations of historical materialism and its socio-psychological effects. But for Georgists (who lack the comfortable support of an academic establishment), the time is always now; they figure they can work out the fine points later.

That could be a mistake. Michael Hudson is one who argues that it is. He notes that Marx's ideas were incorporated into academic discourse on many levels, whereas George's were not, because "At the hands of Marx's followers, historical materialism offered more than just an economic theory or 'tool' as such. It offered an explanatory key to the unfolding of history." Hudson diagnoses the early Georgist movement as suffering from a sort of tunnel vision:

To become a doctrine, economic theory must place itself in the context of the social whole. It must involve a theory of history, of social behavior, and even of intellectual history, for it is natural to think of the whole, and intellectually crippling to think of only the parts... To become a political doctrine in its own right, the theory of rent would have to involve a view of the economy at large, and indeed to become nothing less than a theory of society and of history. It would explain the progress of rent over time, and how the appropriation of rent (and the land's breaking free of taxation) has shaped societies for better or worse, affecting the distribution of income and wealth so as to promote prosperity or poverty. By creating a political doctrine... the

*theory of rent... might have become as fullblown a doctrine in
its own right as Marxist socialism became.* [1]

Now, this strikes me as an intriguing possibility. Suppose Georgism did offer a compelling, richly elucidative theory of history? Good heavens, that would give us stuff for the journals, wouldn't it? I'd like to suggest, as something of a jumping-off point, three issues in Henry George's writings, and our subsequent teaching of them, that point toward an interesting sort of time-consciousness that could, I suspect, grow into a coherent sense, or theory, of history from a Georgist perspective.

These three issues seem nit-picky, mere marginalia in the grand sweep of George's thought—but they stick with the careful reader like pebbles in a shoe. All seemed perfectly sensible, unremarkable things to say in the 1880s, yet for a writer who took as much pride in logical and definitional consistency as Henry George did, they are, nevertheless, a wee bit troubling. They are:
1) Wealth and Services
2) Growth and Progress
3) Skill and Knowledge

Wealth and Services

There has been a long-running debate among Georgist teachers over whether services should be considered as part of production in political economy. George said no. Georgist curricula have for many decades defined political economy as "The science which deals with the nature of wealth and the natural laws governing its production and distribution." Services have no material product, therefore they are not part of production. However, that definition of political economy is incongruous, because labor receives payment, which we call "wages," for providing services, and wages is defined as that part of aggregate wealth that is distributed to the factor we call "labor." If service is not part of production, then the compensation for services has to come from some sub-distribution;

some portion of wealth must be set aside to pay for "non-productive" services. [2] Thus, unlike the provision of pet rocks and snow globes, things like legal or financial services are deemed non-productive.

This leads to pointless complication—yet George resolutely argued it. He was on familiar ground. John Stuart Mill was clear that the science was about the production and distribution of *wealth* (though he spent many pages considering how the "natural law" part of the definition worked itself out). [3] Ricardo was on the same wavelength, stating that "the principal problem in political economy" is determining the laws that regulate the distribution of "the produce of the earth" among the three factors of production.[4] Henry George inherited this traditional conception of things, and it fit in nicely with his paramount concern that *wealth* (physical products of labor) must be distinguished from *land* (natural opportunities). This was important enough that a niggling little inconsistency in the definition of production (and hence the definition of political economy itself) seems trifling—but there it is. Although the Henry George School's introductory course traditionally defines the science of political economy as stated above, I think it's noteworthy that Henry George himself didn't attempt to define "political economy" in *Progress and Poverty*.

He did so in *The Science of Political Economy,* where the issue of wealth and services resurfaces, in a most interesting way. He felt the need to include a chapter titled "Why Political Economy Considers only Wealth." [5] He starts by saying that the traditional definition of political economy is sufficient, but then proceeds to call that statement seriously into question:

> …wealth is not the only result of human exertion, nor is it indeed the final cause of human exertion. That is not reached until wealth is spent or consumed in satisfaction of desire. Wealth itself is in fact only a halting-place or storehouse on the way between prompting desire and final satisfaction; a point at which exertion, journeying towards the satisfaction of desire, remains for a time stored up in concrete form, and

from whence it may be called forth to yield the satisfaction which is its ultimate aim. And there are exertions aiming at the satisfaction of desire which do not pass through the form of wealth at all.

George recognizes that the cause of economic activity is the satisfaction of desire, not merely the production of material goods. So why stick with the incomplete definition? Convention. If he didn't, people might not have known what he was talking about. He concludes that "Political economy has a duty and a province of its own. It is not and it cannot be the science of everything..." Fine, but that fails to explain why political economy should not include functions that, by George's own explanation in this very chapter, clearly fall within its purview.

This minor definitional inconsistency wasn't a big deal, though, even as late as 1897. *Material* progress was still the important thing. That was what was making the great fortunes and supplying the potential for such miraculous improvements in society. Of course political economy was about the production of physical wealth—what else would it be about? Although more and more people were joining the ranks of the proletariat, a great many people still worked on farms, or crafts, or in small stores or businesses. The march of concentration had not yet proceeded to the level of consolidation that would, one day, render people alienated not just from the fruits of their labor but from the very meaning of what they do. Henry George didn't see alienation as part of industrial production itself, as Marx did, but rather as a result of unjust restriction of the workers' economic opportunities.

The Science of Political Economy was left unfinished, and we can't know how he would have revised it, but in writing this chapter (following truth where it led), George was recognizing and exploring (albeit tentatively) an inconsistency which he had inherited from his predecessors. It might have made sense in the mid-19th century to exclude services from the definition of production, but George was seeking natural laws—and on that level, errors can't hide forever.

Another convention that Henry George inherited was the labor theory of value. The term "value" is ubiquitous in Progress and Poverty, yet no definition is offered. The concept of value does get fully—and ingeniously—analyzed in *The Science of Political Economy*. Unfortunately, though, the latter book was unfinished, didn't appear during George's lifetime, and over the years has been read by far fewer people than Progress and Poverty—so, the understanding of "value" that people associate with Henry George is definitely the one put forth in *P&P*. That's unfortunate, because it is expressed there in muddled language that contributes, I suspect, to lingering misconceptions about what Georgist political economy is about.

Generations of *P&P* students have dutifully answered study questions that Henry George's remedy would give workers the full reward of their labor, and capitalists the full return of their capital. They say this because George says it, again and again, in Book IX—but what kind of malarkey is this? George says that laborers and capital owners have not been getting their full rewards, because of the robbery of land monopoly. Now, to be sure, the pre-remedy situation is unfair to workers and capitalists. But the implication is that there exists an amount of wealth, a "full reward" that workers and capitalists are not getting. If this "full reward" exists as a phenomenon in the economy, one would assume that it is calculable—as, indeed, it would be, were the labor theory of value, as propounded by Ricardo (and, later, Marx) to hold true.

Furthermore, if there is such a phenomenon as labor and capital's "full reward," there has to be a similarly identifiable "normal" or non-speculative "rent line," to which the speculative premium is added. This has led some Georgist theorists to separate rent into two components: "rack-rent," an unnaturally high premium on natural opportunities, and "normal" rent, which would remain even after land speculation stopped.

I submit that such lines of reasoning are fruitless and misleading, and spring from a misconception caused by George's momentary carelessness in using the terms current in his day. George goes on to explain how poverty happens, in market-based language of which any modern economist would approve. He notes that the supply of workers is unnaturally increased by the land monopoly's withholding of natural opportunities, and this bids the price of labor down to its marginal cost, which, for workers lacking unusual skills or other bargaining power, is bare subsistence.[6] The raising of wages under the Georgist remedy requires no mythical "full reward"—it is entirely market-based, and will end up where it ends up. The same is true of the "rent line"—indeed, post-remedy rent levels would be further complicated by dynamic forces caused by the remedy itself, processes which George describes powerfully in Book IX of *Progress and Poverty.*[7]

Henry George inherited the labor theory of value, but by the time of *The Science of Political Economy* he had disavowed it, affirming that value is not intrinsic, and depends entirely on the higgling of the market.[8] He does believe in a labor theory of property, however—but that is an entirely different thing, which bears on George's concept of the natural laws of distribution, not on the nature of value.

Growth and Progress

The second issue in our study is closely related to the first. However, the key insight here comes not from George's mistakes, but from a point about which I think he was far ahead of his time. The point is George's refutation—"modification" is probably more accurate—of Adam Smith's assertion that selfishness is at the root of economic behavior. George writes, rather grandiosely,

Shortsighted is the philosophy which counts on selfishness as the master motive of human action. It is blind to facts of which the world is full. It sees not the present, and reads not the past aright. If you would move men to action, to what shall you appeal? Not to their pockets, but to their patriotism; not to selfishness, but to sympathy. (Book IX, Chp. 4)

Here, I think, George's fervent style obscures a truly brilliant piece of analysis that merits scrutiny in today's economic debates. He is saying that economic behavior is properly understood as human beings' efforts to satisfy their desires—whatever those desires may be. We've already discussed how desires are unique to each individual, and how their satisfaction need not be in material form. Here, George adds a sociological note to his basic axiom of economic behavior—a note that leads directly to his conception of what constitutes progress in society. For Henry George, it is "want and fear of want" that causes so much of the negative behavior that plagues society and creates a misanthropic view of human nature. He illustrates this by comparing the behavior around two very different dinner tables: one at a charity soup-kitchen where the food is close to running out, the other in a gracious, comfortable, civilized household. Which example illustrates the norm for human table manners?

The clear implication of this is that if society moves toward a more just and prosperous social order (as it simultaneously maximizes, in George's terms, its association and equality), the kinds of desires that people seek to satisfy will shift in beneficent ways. We already see some evidence of this in certain kinds of self-reinforcing demographic or cultural shifts. It's widely documented, for example, that birth rates decline as living standards and educational levels improve. There are also strong correlations (both positive and negative) between regional prosperity and successful habitat and wildlife conservation. This leads us to suspect that a society that eliminated involuntary unemployment would be transformed in many subtle ways, far beyond the sphere of mere "economics." Jeff Smith envisioned such a shift, in an article provocatively titled "The Protestant Work Ethic vs. the Polynesian Play Ethic." Noting that a nose-to-grindstone approach to making more and better stuff served us well, perhaps, through the industrial revolution, but now, "when we need to shift gears and take advantage of the mechanical miracles we have wrought, a play ethic suits us better." There is a model for such a "play ethic" in Polynesian societies where food is abundant and climate mild:

As much as provide food, men were needed to provide love, to nurture as well as to labor. People esteemed the bearer of glad tidings, the easy-going person with the ready smile for everyone. The quick wit with a joke or story for every occasion earned the respect of his fellows. The one eager to break into song or dance was the one whom others followed. And children were a pleasure. Were a workaholic possible, he would be considered crazy.[9]

The march of material progress—to which *Progress and Poverty* was a direct response—made possible a living just as easy as that of the Polynesians (but, of course, with infinitely more varied possibilities). Realizing this potential would shift our economic behavior—in terms of quantity, to be sure, but, more interestingly, in terms of quality.

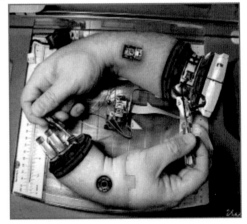

We have a neighbor here in Maine who is an organic farmer. He and his wife sell the meat and vegetables they grow at farmers' markets. They try to minimize their cash flow, but occasionally they take paying jobs when they must. This farmer has a gigantic, beautiful Belgian horse, an animal that is bred to work, and who needs to work to stay healthy. For the last few years, the farmer and the horse have mowed, raked and hauled hay, which the horse ate during the winter. In the winter, the horse has pulled a snowplow to clear their driveway. Now: to what extent can this be meaningfully described as economic behavior? The farmer is, like everyone else, is "satisfying his desires with the least exertion." And, regularly clearing a long driveway of heavy Maine snow is a valuable service (lacking a horse, we pay cash to a guy with a rig). However, can the value of that snow-plowing be computed in terms of the opportunity cost of the market value of this guy's labor? Certainly not; certainly a large part, most, in fact, of the effort our neighbor expended on haying and plowing (and feeding, and hoof-cleaning) has had the character of things he did for his own satisfaction. And yet—and here's where our "Georgist sense of history" starts to come in—he was using the horse to plow his driveway, and that was something that had economic value. Note that I've been describing this activity in the past tense. This year he hasn't been plowing the driveway with his horse. At some marginal point, alas, it became preferable to simply buy hay with a little bit of his cash earnings, and use a truck for plowing. But, although the man's cash flow (and national GDP) increased, his quality of life decreased.

It seems likely that in a more prosperous economy, there would be many more examples of this sort of blending of economic and personal concerns in the choices people make. This sort of blending is manifestly not a feature of industrial society. It is a post-industrial phenomenon. It contains, probably, a harking-back to a romantic conception of simpler times—but without the endless, backbreaking toil. Remember that the wage-slaves of 18th-century textile mills took those jobs, in many cases, because they seemed better then working on farms. Only recently has it become both possible and widely desirable for people to use modern technology to enable them to enjoy the work of farming. The spiritual and ecological pitfalls of industrial farming have started to come home to people. Local, labor-intensive small farming is becoming not only feasible but fashionable. But it is seldom, in strict terms of the bottom line, profitable. It is "profitable" in more ambiguous, personal terms—possibilities that general prosperity allows more people to explore.

Skill and Knowledge

Some years ago, I was brought up short by a question in the Henry George School's course in Economic Science, which asked,  "Which of the two (knowledge and skill) is more important in the development of civilization?" The reading, in *The Science of Political Economy*, admitted a definite answer to that question, in George's words: "It is not in skill, but in the knowledge that can be communicated from one to another, that the civilized man shows his superiority to the savage." (*Book I, Chp. 6*) That is a very interesting sentence from a 21st-century perspective. For one thing, there are lots of thoughtful, well-read people who don't think the accomplishments of "the civilized man" stack up so well against "the savage" at this point in history. But, we shouldn't put this down to a mere lack of political correctness. George goes on to explain in this chapter that "savages" (say, aboriginal people) regularly display skills of various kinds that "civilized man" (say, European colonists) hold in awe. The implication is that modern people, because of their having taken advantage of the results of stored knowledge, have less need to develop skills. Very interesting! This chapter hints at, but ultimately rejects, an important insight. Indeed, George has been down this interesting path before, in the passages discussed above, among others. But here, in his attempt to nail down the eternal nature and processes of civilization, he couldn't let his imagination run free.

Nowadays, this process has played itself out; we've come all the way around to the other side of the question. Society's reliance on applied knowledge has brought about vast levels of abstraction (and all manner of labor-saving gadgetry). But it has left people disempowered. Modern life is seen as a collection of specialties. One aspires to learn a specialty in order to make a good living, which enables one to hire other specialists—to prepare frozen food, fix faulty wiring and treat emotional problems. Left on our own, having worked for years to master a specialty, we find ourselves so without skills that we must depend on roadside assistance, summoned via cell-phone, should a tire go flat, or fuel run out. Our farmer neighbor was compelled by hard economic realities to trade a satisfying activity that demanded a wide range of well-practiced skills for a mind-numbing daily stint in a retail establishment. And what's the first thing many hard-working middle-class people do when they retire? Why, they take up a hobby—or resume an artistic pursuit that they'd set aside in order to make a living. They do something, in other words, which requires the oh-so-satisfying acquisition of skill.

These little anachronistic snippets of Henry George's thought are worth our attention for a couple of reasons. For one, they afford an interesting perspective on how our thinking about these elements of economic life change over the years. What's more important for our study, though, is how they rebound in ways that strengthen the basic Georgist thesis. Nikki Giovanni once whimsically proclaimed, "I am so hip even my errors are correct"—and in a sense this is true of these little "errors" of Henry George's. Yes, services are rightly understood as part of production—and, by golly, look what aspect of production becomes progressively more important as society reaches an advanced stage of material progress! [10] Knowledge can perhaps be seen as more important to civilization than skill—but only for a certain stage in the history of material progress, after which skill begins to come into its own once more. And it's only too clear that economic growth cannot, any longer, simply mean a piling-up of *stuff*—but, rather, an ever-more subtle and intricate satisfaction of *desires*.

The evolution of land tenure systems plays a key role in the historical process, too—but that is so clear in George's writings and in Georgist thought generally that it need only be mentioned here. In early times, when traditional societies roam over plenty of land, and skills are economically paramount, communal land tenure is the order of things. Feudalism, in various forms, marks a transitional stage, in which the economic utility of exclusive tenure of

An Outline

What's emerging here is a picture of a continuum of social development. We might be able to outline its stages—in a glib, sketchy, preliminary way—as follows:

PRE-AGRARIAN — traditional societies; communal land tenure; skill overshadows knowledge in production; traditional, tribal government.

AGRARIAN — private tenure recognized, but production tied to the land; commons still important; traditional values and skills still important, but new efficiencies lead to increased surplus; monarchic government.

EARLY INDUSTRIAL — private ownership assured; division of labor and economies of scale become important; artisanal and small farm production still widely practiced, but decreasing; movement toward democratic government.

FULL INDUSTRIAL — workers in proletarian role; industrial power enables great class disparity; knowledge overshadows skill; landless workers bid wages downward; corrupt democratic government leads to revolutionary pressures.

POST-INDUSTRIAL TRANSITION — adjustments made to preserve system; middle class becomes dominant political force; alternative life-styles explored; rebellious social responses to alienation; states respond to economic unrest with social democratic reforms, socialist systems, and/or repressive regimes; mixed economy in which the role of land is hidden.

FULL POST-INDUSTRIAL — environmentalism becomes very important; demographic shifts; information economy; skill and knowledge either integrate or are at war; industrial production is either clean & green, or outsourced to poor countries; the age will be either golden or dark   **— L. D.**

land starts to be understood, but common rights are still widely held. With industrialism comes absolute private property in land, the financial manipulation of its rent, and the dire social and economic pathologies that ensue.

And in the post-industrial society? Perhaps civilization will fail, and a new dark age will ensue. That is by no means impossible—but I see no need to waste time envisioning it, because, among other reasons, Henry George describes it quite sufficiently (*See P&P, Book X, Chp. 4*). However, George didn't give us an adequate picture of a *successful* post-industrial society. That's for us to work out. I hope I've made an intriguing preliminary case, at least, for how a Georgist notion of history can be a guide toward creating a sane set of options for civilization's future.

~ *Georgist Journal* #114
September 2012

End Notes

1. Michael Hudson, "The Theory of Rent Needs a Theory of History," *Land and Liberty*, Winter, 1997.

2. George intimates this in a footnote in *Progress and Poverty*, Book 1, Chp. 3, in the context of his refutation of the wages-fund theory, saying that the payment for a service, such as that of a shoe-shine, comes not from capital, but from wealth one devotes to one's own satisfaction. (One can nevertheless observe that the payment for the shoe-shine is not charity; it it is given in exchange for a desirable thing. Since George defines exchange as part of production, the service would seem to fall in that category.)

3. Mill, John Stuart, *Essays on Some Unsettled Questions of Political Economy*, Second Edition, Batoche Books, Kitchener, 2000.

4. Ricardo, David, *On the Principles of Political Economy and Taxation*, at http://www.econlib.org/library/Ricardo/ricP.html

---

5. Book II, Chp. 28, in the original edition (Robert Schalkenbach Foundation, 1992); Part II, Chp. 14 in the abridged (RSF, 2004).

6. The market for unskilled labor in a non-Georgist modern economy is the only true example of the theoretical ideal that economists call "perfect competition." See:
www.politicaleconomy.org/competition.htm

7. Some—notably, Michael Hudson in the article quoted above—have argued that an accounting of the magnitude of rent in the current economy would be a powerful tool for Georgist advocacy, and that significant resources should be devoted to creating such studies. However that may be, Henry George explains clearly, in Book IX of *Progress and Poverty,* how and why the aggregate rent in a Georgist economy would be very different than it is today, and would change in complex ways that are impossible to predict in advance.

8. He contends that the value of a thing is universally measured in terms of the irksome toil, or labor, it saves its possessor—but, since each individual's idea of what constitutes "labor" is subjective, the economic value that depends on that measure is also subjective.

9. Paper delivered at the Eastern Economic Association conference in New York, 2005.

10. Although "services" are conventionally thought to be a function of labor, labor is not the only factor that can provide the direct satisfaction of human desires. Land and capital can, as well. For example, the economic role of "ecosystem services" has become an important area of study and advocacy in recent years.

— Chapter 11 —

Closing the Virtual Frontier (Redux)

The issue of "Net Neutrality" has been somewhat shoved to the back burner by the more pressing economic concerns of deep unemployment and financial crisis—but it has exercised many people, for some years now, and it isn't going away. What is it about? Why would we be talking about it in the *Georgist Journal*?

The "information superhighway" of the Internet has changed our world in so many ways that it has become hard to remember (or, for our kids, to imagine) life without it. Its rate of growth has been mind-bending by any measure: number of users, commercial importance, journalistic and scholarly attention, hours of our time devoted to it. It has had a "wild frontier" character that has made billionaires out of the geeks who thought up things like Google, Ebay, PayPal, Facebook and Twitter. For a while there it seemed as though just about any Net enterprise would make money—but then things calmed down a bit; around the turn of the century, the Internet settled down to simply being ubiquitous and indispensable. Interestingly, that was about the time that "Net Neutrality" started to become a controversial issue. You see, the neat thing about the Internet is that from the very start, it has been a "many to many" medium. Some sites and services might have become wildly popular, but they all started out with the same access to the same Net as every other. At the end of 2009 there were 234 million websites and 126 million blogs on the Internet.[1]

The universality and wide-open character of the Internet was, really, a happy accident of its design. I wrote about this in 1995:

The Internet started out as a free public good—indeed, as arguably the single most important by-product of US military spending. It started out as the ARPAnet, whose original mission was to provide a command-and-control network that was so hyper-redundant that it could not be disabled. The basic design was for a network that could still function even if huge chunks of it (the Washington, DC and New York metro areas, say) were vaporized in a nuclear war. Thus, packet-switching communications technology was born.[2]

This technology ended up serving purposes that were (thank goodness) quite different from what it was designed for. Yes, it was an efficient means for exchanging information—but people soon realized that this TCP-IP network was far more than that. In fact, it represented a whole new way of communicating. Douglas Adams explained this in his fascinating essay, "The Four Ages of Sand." [3]

Adams said that we humans had always had one-to-one communication, of course, from the very dawn of humanity. Eventually we became adept at one-to-many communication, such as was practiced by Greek orators and was greatly accelerated by the printing press. In time, we started experimenting, in a halting, flawed manner, with many-to-one communication in the form of democratic institutions. But never, until the Internet, did we have the potential for many-to-many communication. It was a whole new way for human beings to exchange information.

The technical reason for this amazing potential was a happy accident. To achieve the capacity to get messages from Washington, DC to Boston, despite the physical absence of the Greater New York Metropolitan Area, the network had to be 100% "dumb." Messages were broken up into packets of data by the Internet Protocol (IP) software, digitally addressed, like little envelopes, and sent off to bounce around the Net through whatever path was open to them. When they reached their destination, they would be reassembled and displayed. It was impossible to know exactly what path the packets of your message would follow during the milliseconds that they went bouncing through the Net. In achieving a network that would function even after large segments of its central trunk were vaporized, we'd also created a network on which each user had exactly the same access as every other user.

Therefore, the Internet also presented an economic problem that wasn't so new: the "tragedy of the commons." The year I wrote my paper, 1995, turned out to be an historic one for the Internet: it was the year that the Federal government stopped funding the NSFnet, the fiber-optic threaded supercomputing centers that formed the "backbone" of the Net. Additional capacity had been provided by universities and research facilities. But, now the Internet was becoming the Next Big Thing, and demand would soar.

Indeed, this brought about the "dot com bubble," which led, among many other things, to telecommunications companies investing in backbone facilities. The profitability of that investment, however, was always doubtful. As the number of Internet users soared in the early 2000s, demand was robust enough for telcos to simply re-sell Internet access to service providers. Now, though, demand for individual internet-access accounts seems to have plateaued—while the bandwidth desired by each user is rapidly increasing.

Why don't the telecommunications folks just build more capacity to handle the load? The short answer is that if a company builds a new backbone facility, it is open for use by every user on the whole Net—not just the ones who pay for it. Early attempts, by companies such as CompuServe and America Online, to restrict users to "home" content were an utter failure. Those companies ended up as regular portals to the open Internet. If the entire Net is open, why would one want to buy access to just a segment of it? But—if the entire Net is open, how can one recoup private investment in what is, by its nature, a public resource?

Congestion has become a serious problem on the Internet, and it looks to get worse. Dire predictions started being made about two years ago that without considerable investment in new backbone facilities, traffic would start to reach the limits of existing capacity by, about: now. Internet "brownouts" are hard to unambiguously identify because of the great variety of local variables—but no one thinks that broadband access, today, is all that it should be, and average connection speed in the United States currently ranks 31st in the world. [4]

The obvious solution to the return-on-investment question

—if it could be accomplished technically—would be to monopolize the Internet's infrastructure in such a way as to ensure high-quality delivery of your content to customers, wherever they might be on the Internet. But how can that be done, in an end-to-end, packet-switched, "dumb network"?

You had to figure that eventually somebody would find a way. You've noticed, haven't you, that streaming video, audio—and commercials—are clearer, sharper and more reliable from big media outlets than from small websites? This is being accomplished by the use of edge-server caching technology, whose leading provider is a hot new company called Akamai. For fees that are affordable for outfits like J. C. Penney, Fox Sports or MTV—but not to folks like the *Henry George Institute*, or thousands of small businesses hoping to sell their wares on the Web—Akamai's systems pull content from its original server and copy it, dynamically as required by traffic needs, to proprietary servers near cities, places with high volumes of end-user traffic. This system dramatically improves performance, and this is especially noticeable in the case of the biggest bandwidth-hog on the Net, streaming video. Unlike email or basic Web pages, for which a half—second delay is no problem, streaming content requires smoothly uninterrupted delivery. [5]

Edge-server caching provides this—but, so far anyway, at too high a price for small players. Will competitors come into this booming market and bring prices down—perhaps making edge-server caching as commonplace as DSL lines? Well, probably not anytime soon. Much of Akamai's technology is patented. It has already won three lawsuits against would-be competitors, and has recently filed a fourth against a startup named Cotendo. [6]

So we're left with the situation that new capacity will only be provided if the provider can own that capacity; and charge for its exclusive use. Looks like we really are seeing a "Closing of the Virtual Frontier." Back in '95, I envisioned an Internet in which big players could build themselves high-capacity proprietary pipes for their own content...

Everyone gets a taste, apparently: those who can afford to pay for priority service can get near-instant transmission; those with less money can still use internet services, paying in the form of delay. Providers of large-bandwidth information services would clearly be happy with such a system. Receivers of large-bandwidth applications would too…

Only one group of internet users is left in the cold in this scenario: the small-scale internet publisher. Up until now, one of the most important defining characteristics of the internet was that everyone has the same access. Sky Cries Mary [a 90s Grunge band from Seattle] can perform a video concert to the same audience as the Rolling Stones. Any small dissident 'zine can command (potentially) as large an audience on the World Wide Web as a major national publication. This is a vital fact about the way the internet has grown and a pervasive aspect of its character (upon which much of its current marketability depends). But if NBC, say, can afford to pay whatever it costs to make its web page zip through to web-browsers, while the local nonprofits, community groups (or geeks-in-basements) get squeezed further and further into the netherworld of delay. To use congestion pricing to incentivize development of information superhighway infrastructure could do irrevocable harm to the two-way character of the internet.

Indeed, many people who are concerned with the rights of privacy and free expression in cyberspace are very troubled by this possibility, and many feel that the only way the open, democratic character of the internet can be preserved is by maintaining it as a public good…

That was fifteen years ago, and that spirit has re-emerged today in the "Net Neutrality" movement.

This can all get rather abstruse. Let's quickly sum up what we've seen so far—and then get to what Georgist theory might have to offer toward a solution. The original nature of the Internet was a "dumb network," an end-to-end medium in which every user had the same access to network resources as every other user. This "many-to-many" communication model offered great incentives for innovation and—changed our world. The great increase in demand for Internet resources cannot be supplied in a free market unless investors can be guaranteed the exclusive use of the new capacity they provide. But if they secure that exclusive access while providing content to users of the Internet, they are effectively walling off portions of a public resource for their own profit! It should be noted that these huge video files go to the edge-servers, and go from the edge-servers to the end users, via the same Internet we all use—but it is the proprietary use of these servers that makes them worth paying for, because users get to see stuff clearly, crisply, and without interruption.

Skeptics in the net-neutrality debate wonder why all this is a problem. Companies, they say, are offering to sell users an enhanced experience of the Web. Should they not expect to be paid for this? Conventional economic theory does have such considerations as antitrust policy informed by analyzing various levels of imperfect competition, but it's a highly complex matter that affords no categorical answers. Georgist theory claims to be able to do better. Is it possible to look at the net-neutrality issue in terms of the factors of production, and identify what rent, if any, is being generated?

Additional physical capacity for the Net, whether communal or proprietary, is clearly "capital" in Georgist terms; there's no doubt about that. But what about the Internet itself? Isn't it also just a collection of physical equipment that carries bits of data here and there? It looks that way—but if so, then why all this talk about monopolizing and enclosing? There's something about the Internet that seems very land-like.

That perception is a sound one, I think, and it arises from two facts about the Internet: 1) that it was initially established and maintained by the community and was freely available to all users on an equal basis; and 2) the Internet exhibits a positive network externality: in other words, the more people use it, the more valuable it is to each user. This naturally-occurring process, applied to something that started out as a free public good, created a natural opportunity for the users of the Internet. It was, in Georgist terms, "land at the margin." It was free to all, [7] and the marginal cost of sending a piece of data across the Net was zero. But wait a minute. When we talk about land monopoly, we talk about the monopolization of unique, addressable spaces. What space was getting monopolized on the Internet? Doesn't the Net transcend space, allowing everybody to interact in real time with everybody else? Perhaps. But Henry George, in *The Science of Political Economy*, reminds us that the natural limitations on production happen not just in space, but also in time. As the demands for bandwidth increase, and especially as more and more users want streaming applications that don't tolerate delays, we find that time is the important limiting factor in the economy of the Internet. By providing the means to assure that proprietary content gets to users without delay, Akamai and similar firms are effectively monopolizing particular, valuable bits of time.

Georgist theory goes on to assert that a natural opportunity acquires value due to the actions of the entire community, and its value will be equal to the cost of maintaining the community's infrastructure that creates it. In this case, the rent is the fees paid to providers of edge-servers to enable high QoS [8] in bandwidth-intensive applications to end users. These fees are high enough to elicit considerable investment in R&D and expensive equipment. Indeed, some commentators predict that mirroring edge-server technology will become the norm for the entire Internet someday. But that won't happen while the technology for delivering it is exclusive, and its owners can charge a toll for its use — use which, unavoidably, places congestion-load demands on the entire Internet.

So what's the remedy? The standard net-neutrality position today would be to outlaw practices that lead to time-privatization on the Net [9] — but opponents scream, rightly, that this amounts to outlawing innovation. [10]

What would a Georgist solution to this conundrum look like? Suppose we made a national decision to beef up everyone's broadband access to the same level as those who now pay for the high speeds provided by Akamai's equipment. That would put folks like Akamai out of business, probably—and the public might have to buy out their current interest. However, rent that big media companies are willing to pay for such access could be reinvested in increased capacity. Users willing to pay for extra-high speeds could still get them, but rather than incentivizing a self-limiting exclusivity, the profits gained therefrom could go toward making such services much more affordable—perhaps even free.

What would that mean, in the real world? It would mean nothing less than a realization of the idealistic early vision of the World Wide Web: that people with important things to say via the Internet would be free to say them as powerfully as they could—limited by nothing but their own imaginations.

We may be wise to distrust our knowledge: and, unless we have tested them, to distrust what we may call our reasonings: but never to distrust reason itself.
– Henry George, *The Science of Political Economy*

~ Georgist Journal #116
January 2011

End Notes

1. www.royal.pingdom.com offers a fascinating, documented compilation of Net stats.

2. This paper surveyed the then-current literature on the Internet and its future. Much of its analysis was based on Henry George's The Science of Political Economy.

3. This appeared in Adams's posthumous book The Salmon of Doubt, and is available on the Web.

4. www.speedtest.net

5. http://paidcontent.org/article/419-akamais-patent-lawsuit-likely-to-be-a-giantheadache-for-startup-cotend/

6. In other words it requires what those in the trade call "low latency" or a high guaranteed QoS (quality of service).

7. Users had to pay local providers for access to the Internet, but such charges were for the equipment and services used in gaining access, not for the use of the Net itself.

8. a.k.a. "Quality of Service," the standard term for the level of delay free performance of streaming content.

9. For example, in the proposed the Internet Freedom Preservation Act of 2009 (H.R. 3458), Internet providers shall "not provide or sell to any content, application, or service provider, including any affiliate provider or joint venture, any offering that prioritizes traffic over that of other such providers on an Internet access service..."

10. See, for example, papers by Tim Wu and Chris Yoo, linked at: http://timwu.org/network_neutrality.html

Chapter 12

Nobody's Occupying THIS Lot

One small block west of the main Liberty Plaza headquarters of the Occupy Wall Street demonstration sits the lot at 133 Greenwich Street. If the Occupiers have a few free moments, they might want to check it out. It sold last year for $19.6 million, or $3,208 per square foot, and nothing has been happening on it for

quite some time. The annual property tax bill for this parcel is $189,839. That seems like a fair amount of money, but evidently it has not been enough to stimulate the development of this extremely valuable site. That isn't surprising: interest rates are low these days, but a meager 4% return on $19.6 million still amounts to $784,000. The long-term rate of return on this investment is much higher, of course, for despite the current downturn, the owner certainly expects the lot's value to appreciate.

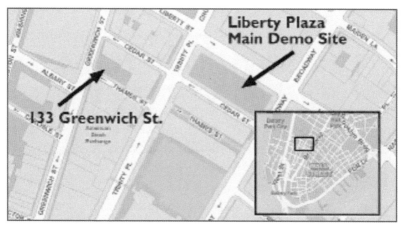

Liberty Plaza
Main Demo Site

133 Greenwich St.

In the five boroughs of New York City there are 33,142 vacant lots—a total area of 23.9 square miles. This downtown Manhattan lot is classed as commercial real estate. For the last five years, the "full market value" that the city reports for such parcels has averaged 23.3% of what such lots eventually sell for.

Housing is very expensive in New York—as in many other cities, and jobs are hard to come by. Might housing be more reasonable, and employment more abundant, if warehoused sites such as this were put to productive use? Taxpayers provide the infrastructure and services that make lots like this so valuable. Meanwhile, real estate speculators do nothing, for years, and reap huge rewards.

Here's the building next door. Its annual property tax bill is $485,154.

~ *Georgist Journal* #118
September 2011

— Chapter 13 —

Defining Political Economy

Definitions were extremely important to Henry George. A great
deal of his writing was devoted to making sure his readers had
clear, consistent terms to use. His paramount concern, of course, was
to functionally distinguish wealth (a product of human labor) from
land (natural opportunities independent of human action). If the
reader has been with us all along, that distinction will be familiar and
obvious. As a strong believer in neat definitional boundaries, George
gave the study of political economy itself the same treatment, defining
it as "the science which treats of the nature of wealth and the natural
laws governing its production and distribution." This is the standard
definition that has been used over the years in Georgist curriculum—
for example in a familiar bookmark, listing basic economic definitions, used for decades by students of the Henry George School.

Yet, as you may have noticed, the *Henry George Institute* no longer
uses that definition. We have defined political economy more inclu-
sively (and, alas, in a few more words), as "the science which deals with
the nature of economic value and the natural laws governing the production and distribution of valuable goods and services."

Does this "new" definition seem nit-picky? Untidy? Perhaps.
However, it encompasses an aspect of production that, while it may
have seemed mere marginalia in Henry George's day, has become vital
in the 21st century: the concept of services. And, along the way, it
leads us to a more comprehensive, elucidative definition of political
economy.

If political economy is thought to encompass only the production
and distribution of physical wealth, then services—in which human
desires are satisfied directly, without the exchange of a physical product—cannot be part of production. Henry George seems to take this
position, in a footnote in *Progress and Poverty* (*Book I, Chp. 3*), saying
that the payment for a service, such as that of a shoeshine, comes not

from capital, but from wealth one devotes to one's own satisfaction. However, the payment for the shoeshine is not charity; it is given in exchange for a desirable thing. Since George defines exchange as part of production, the service would fall in that category.

In *The Science of Political Economy*, Henry George explains how and why the fundamental purpose of economic behavior is not the production of physical goods, but rather the satisfaction of human desires. He applies the term "service" to the process of human labor aimed toward the satisfaction of desire, and explains that wealth is service embodied in material form. Wealth can be transported or exchanged, until it serves its ultimate purpose of being consumed—of satisfying human desire. George reminds us that "wealth itself is in fact only a halting-place or storehouse on the way between prompting desire and final satisfaction... And there are exertions aiming at the satisfaction of desire which do not pass through the form of wealth at all." (*Book II, Chp. 18*) The accepted term for such exertions, for George as well as for modern writers, is "services."

Why is this important? It isn't bad, to begin with, to remove a logical flaw, especially when it does no violence to George's basic thesis. More important, though, it steers our analysis clear of a 21st-century danger zone. If political economy is the science of the production and distribution of wealth, and wealth is inescapably material, that suggests that economic growth is inevitably the production and distribution of *more material*—with the attendant using-up and fouling-up of increasingly scarce natural resources. This rings many an alarm bell today. We're warned that economic growth cannot continue on a finite planet—and if it does, sooner or later we will face a catastrophic, Malthusian collapse.

While it is well, in any case, to address the environmental costs of material growth and pollution, we don't need to fundamentally redesign the science of political economy to do so. That is because the true goal of economic activity, as Henry George reminds us, is not the creation of more material stuff; it is the satisfaction of human desires. Modern production creates a whole lot of stuff that nobody wants. These days, one desire that people are willing to pay to have satisfied is for clean and sustainable production. In other words, people are willing to pay to get what they want with less net resource-depletion and pollution. More and more, people are willing to pay for production that ends up producing not more stuff, but less stuff—remembering that pollution, after all, is also stuff that gets paid for, somewhere, sometime, by somebody: it isn't free.

This way of looking at things gives services a new prominence in political economy. To see how and why, we should remember that labor (such as that of shoeshine boys, or lawyers) isn't the only economic factor that can directly satisfy desires. Capital can, too; examples include the satisfactions provided by elevators, automatic car-washing machines or public rest rooms. And land offers a category of direct satisfactions that have recently generated great interest: "ecosystem services." The capacity of the air and the sea, for example, to absorb pollutants and render them harmless to us has, for a long time, been taken as a free service—but in recent years its value has grown a great deal.

Here, then, is an area of distribution—the rents due to ecosystem services—that is an important part of political economy, and yet would be completely missed, were our study restricted to the production and distribution of physical wealth. That seems ample reason to move beyond our old definition of the science of political economy.

Now at this point, some might ask: If your Institute can't even accept Henry George's definition of the science itself, why still use his book? Doesn't this reveal George's analysis to be hopelessly obsolete?

Not for a moment! One minor logical inconsistency cannot invalidate the profound insights that Henry George articulates with such clarity and force. Indeed, by insisting on the distinct role of land as a factor of production, George's ideas lay indispensable groundwork for the field that has since come to be known as "ecological economics."

In *The Science of Political Economy*, Henry George sought to lay out the basic principles and natural laws of the science itself—before and beneath the complications and adulterations that have overlaid it, and which form the bulk of what passes, today, for economic analysis. For example, today, great ink is spilled and vast numbers crunched over the boom-bust cycle—economic volatility, the inflation/unemployment tradeoff, etc.—yet Henry George gave us not a single sentence on the topic in *The Science of Political Economy* ! At first glance that might seem quaint, archaic, a postcard from a simpler era. But, of course, George himself was deeply concerned with the boom/bust cycle. He ignored it in this book because he believed it had nothing to do with the natural laws of production and distribution. It is an entirely curable social affliction, if only those laws are clearly observed and applied. For one more example: modern students might think to fault George because his book appears to offer no discussion of "externalities." But, of course, that isn't so. Though he didn't use the term, Henry George was a pioneer in the analysis of externalities. He described in detail the external effects of land speculation, private collection of community-created land rent, public confiscation of producers' legitimately-earned wages and interest—as well as lesser influences such as protective tariffs, labor unions and public debts. Indeed, without settling (as George sought to) the moral question of what legitimately belongs to the community, and to individuals—how can one even say what "externalities" are external *to*?

Henry George himself, after all, insists that readers not take his word for anything, but follow truth where it may lead. Yet we believe, with George, that there are natural laws of political economy—and until another writer comes along who articulates those natural laws with greater eloquence and clarity, we'll keep offering Henry George's works to new students.

This essay is part of the supplemental readings for the HGI's course in Economic Science (www.politicaleconomy.org).

~ *Georgist Journal* #119
April 2012

Chapter 14

How to Break the Curse

In 1855 Chief Seattle of the Suquamish tribe in the Puget Sound region gave a speech in response to a request from President Franklin Pierce that his tribe sell its ancestral lands to the government.

A speech that we thought was Chief Seattle's was commemorated on Earth Day and made into a famous childrens' book. That speech was an environmentalist manifesto in which Seattle agrees to sell the land, if the white man will always respect the earth, and "treat the beasts of the land and the birds of the sky as his brothers." It was a stirring call to honor and respect the natural world—but, alas, it was not what Seattle said. It was penned in 1971 by a screenwriter named Ted Perry—who, reportedly, was appalled that his fictional speech was mistaken for the original.

And when you think about it—it did seem a bit fishy, didn't it? We'll sell you our sacred land, if you promise to be a good environmental steward?

In the real speech, Chief Seattle made it clear that he had no intention of letting white people off the hook. He would only relinquish the land because he had no other choice. "Your God," he said, "loves your people and hates mine... He has abandoned his red children… Now we are orphans. There is no one to help us."

Seattle went on to say that he would "sell" the land if his people would "always be allowed to visit the graves of our fathers and our friends." These words cannot be taken at face value, because that condition was impossible: Seattle explained, in the clearest terms, that the graves of his fathers and his friends encompassed the entire North American continent.

> …at evening the forests are dark with the presence of the dead. When the last red man has vanished from this earth… these shores will still swarm with the invisible dead of my people… There is no place in this country where a man can be alone. At night when the streets of your towns and cities are quiet, and you think they are empty, they will throng with the returning spirits that once thronged them, and that still love those places. The white man will never be alone. So let him be just and deal kindly with my people.

I believe that Seattle was right. Private ownership of land, in the sense of absolute private ownership or "alienation" of land, is not really possible; it's a myth—and society clings to that myth at its peril.

Land is the entire material world; boundaries are arbitrary and impermanent. One cannot have title or tenure to land per se, but only to a bounded piece of it. Legally, what land ownership amounts to is the title to a bundle of rights that attaches to a spe-

In a deeper sense, we can see that Chief Seattle was warning us that the alienation of land leads to personal, spiritual alienation. Does "owning" your land make it possible for you to be alone on it? Can you forbid access to every trespasser, forever? You think you can be alone on your land, because you can defend it with your gun. But on some level, you know that everyone has an equal right to that land. If you don't compensate the community for your exclusive privilege to it, then your sovereign ownership can never be secure. Seattle didn't lay this curse on us—he just pointed it out.

Woody Guthrie seemed to agree, in this less-known verse from his most famous song:

> *As I went walking I saw a sign there*
> *And on the sign it said "No Trespassing."*
> *But on the other side it didn't say nothing,*
> *That side was made for you and me.*

"This machine kills fascists." ~ Woody Guthrie

In the last section of *Progress and Poverty*, Henry George addressed the question of how societies decline, or advance. He asked, "What is the law of social progress?" Such a law, he wrote, must explain clearly and definitely... why, though mankind started presumably with the same capacities and at the same time, there now exist such wide differences in social development. It must account for the arrested civilizations and for the decayed and destroyed civilizations... for retrogression as well as for progression... it must show us what are the essential conditions of progress, and what social adjustments advance and retard it.

Following logically from all of his previous analysis, George identified two essential conditions of social progress: **association** and **equality.**

cific location. What rights are in that bundle is subject to society's legal control.

Equality is something we all have a fairly clear idea of. But asked, "What is the law of social progress?" Such a law, he wrote,

> *must explain clearly and definitely... why, though mankind started presumably with the same capacities and at the same time, there now exist such wide differences in social development. It must account for the arrested civilizations and for the decayed and destroyed civilizations... for retrogression as well as for progression... it must show us what are the essential conditions of progress, and what social adjustments advance and retard it.*

Following logically from all of his previous analysis, George identified two essential conditions of social progress: association and equality.

Equality is something we all have a fairly clear idea of. But what did he mean by "association"?

Association is nothing less than the basis for all the efficiencies that flow from a free market economy. People come together into towns and cities; they cooperate, and compete, and the whole community is better off. People write, and speak, create music and art and publish their works, and everyone learns. To see the great power of free association, consider its absence. Soviet Russia was a society that worked to inhibit association. Freedom of the press and religion were severely curtailed; economic decisions were made by central committees and could not be opposed. The Soviet Union had great political and military power, but it couldn't stand the weight of its own inefficiency and repression.

Similarly, a society that inhibits equality is in all kinds of trouble. It ill-treats the people it keeps down, of course—but even the fortunate few must waste precious time and effort maintaining an unjust status quo. The more unequal a society is, the more effort it takes to maintain it. Probably the most obviously unequal society was the American institution of slavery. Yet there have been—and sadly, still are—many societies that keep women in a second-class state of oppression and servitude.

To the extent that a society encourages, honors and maintains equality and association, it moves forward. And to the extent that a society hinders or represses those things, it declines. That, according to Henry George, is the law of human progress.

The institution of private ownership of land works against both equality and association. If some people are granted exclusive ownership of the land, while others must pay private owners for access to it, that is the very antithesis of equality. And private landowners powerfully inhibit association by choosing to hold valuable land out of use. That means that the Georgist remedy is essential for sustainable social progress.

The Amazing Disappearing Land!

A highly-skilled stage magician can make something huge—the Statue of Liberty, say—seem to disappear. Yet if that magician were to actually start to believe in his own smoke and mirrors, our feelings about his performance would shift from awe to pity. Modern economics has performed the astounding trick of making land disappear from economic analysis. And, alas, many have come to believe in their own illusion.

If you had never thought about land as a separate factor, of course, then its absence from economic consideration wouldn't ring any bells. People have been trained to ignore the meaning of land—and ignore it they do.

This has profound consequences. Let's consider a few examples.

If private ownership of land is sacrosanct, then:

Malthus was right. The poor will indeed be with us always—and they will always breed faster than food can be grown. The urbanization of the poor south will continue, and misery will grow. Poor people keep being born, and there just isn't enough land to go around. Transnational corporations have every right to retain their vast holdings, on which they pay local peasants starvation wages to grow crops

for export.

If private ownership of land is sacrosanct, then:

Keynes was right. The boom/bust cycle can never be eliminated, only managed by fiddling with fiscal and monetary policy, which grows less effective over time. Inflation will always overheat before all the willing and able workers can find jobs; taxation will always place a dead weight on production. Real estate speculators have every right to enjoy the appreciation of their assets; it's their due, fair pay for entrepreneurial acumen.

If private ownership of land is sacrosanct, then:

Marx was right. In the "capitalist" system, there is an inherent structural tendency for the rich to get richer and the poor to get poorer. Labor's gains via legislation or collective bargaining will always erode, as real wages inexorably drop. Those at the top will re-sort to ever-more-drastic repressive measures to keep disgruntled workers in line. As the inefficiencies and dead weights of the system grow, regimes will resort to imperialistic wars to secure resources and profit margins.

If private ownership of land is sacrosanct, then:

There really is a global "race to the bottom." Nothing can be done to provide better opportunities for poor workers in developing countries. They need the work—at whatever pay their faceless employers are willing to give them. If nations want to develop at all, they have to play by rules set by multinational corporations. Land barons in those nations have no incentive to let go of their holdings to give workers better options. Why should they do that? It's their land.

And finally: if private ownership of land is sacrosanct, then:

Dick Cheney was right. Terrorism will continue to escalate. People who resent our advantages and hate what we stand for will become increasingly desperate and dangerous, and we must do what's necessary to protect ourselves. Our very way of life depends on control over scarce oil, water and cropland.

Fortunately, we now know that private ownership of land need not be sacrosanct. The alternative is not only viable but infinitely preferable. We can replace of burdensome, invasive taxes with public collection of rent. Doing so would confer a smörgasbord of benefits on society, without compromising the efficiency of a free-market economy.

At one time, slavery was deemed a sensible, sound practice; it's even condoned in the Bible. At one time, it was taken for granted that women had no rights beyond what their fathers and husbands chose to grant them.

Nevertheless, through the long years when such backward practices held sway, there were always thoughtful individuals who saw the denial of basic human rights for what it was. The most basic right of all is that of life itself—yet, if private land ownership is sacrosanct, then we are obliged to pay a landowner for access to the natural resources that we must have in order to live.

In *Progress and Poverty*, Henry George thundered, "Private property in land is a bold, bare, enormous wrong, like to chattel slavery."

So far, most people have been either too busy, too fearful — or too well-served by the status quo — to stop and think about the truth of those words. But they will. Eventually it will dawn on them that nothing else will work.

~ Georgist Journal #128

Adapted from the script of the final segment in a new 16-part video series sponsored by the Henry George School and narrated by the author.

Original artwork by Bob Clancy

— Chapter 15 —

On Fictitious Commodities, and Sacred Land

It's very likely that we Georgists will keep trying to "diagnose our failure" until society finally adopts the Georgist remedy.[1] One chestnut that's resurfaced recently is the notion that our focus on the land monopoly, while OK as far as it goes, naively ignores other modern evils that do just as much damage. In particular, some Georgist circles have been abuzz about Karl Polanyi's contention that land, labor and money are really "fictitious commodities" which must not be given over to the cruel, callous Invisible Hand of the market.[2]

I've been trying to wrap my mind around the idea that land, labor and money are not to be "commodified." What is a commodity? I think we can synthesize various definitions to say that a commodity is something that is voluntarily exchanged, in arms-length transactions, for other valuable things. "Arms length" is a key phrase, because such exchanges don't have to depend on familiarity or personal trust; obviously, this greatly expands the field on which exchanges can be made, expanding the synergistic benefits therefrom. This is the familiar logic that undergirds the market economy.

Karl Polanyi, on the other hand, didn't believe that the market economy can be trusted. He argued that if land, labor and money—parts of the economy that are utterly essential to our well-being—are left to the market, society will proceed inexorably toward debasement and ruin.

What sort of things, then, should be "commodified"? Well, widgets—hula hoops, toasters, things like that; it would be permissible to have a free market in capital and consumer goods. Yet, it's hard to see how such a market could be "free" in any meaningful sense if its most vital inputs, labor and capital, as well as its medium of exchange, were subject to government control. Nevertheless, that seems to have been where Polanyi was leading us. He did not envision a planned economy a la Karl Marx. He was a big fan of Franklin D. Roosevelt's New Deal; he wanted capitalism to fix itself with a vibrant public sector and a social-democratic welfare state.

In the United States, post-WWII prosperity exhibited many elements that Polanyi would have approved of. The G.I. Bill facilitated widespread home ownership. The Interstate Highway System and other public works expanded public infrastructure. Union membership was strong, peaking around 1955; college graduation rates steadily climbed. Marginal tax rates were high (unthinkably high by today's standards), with a top rate of over 90% as late as 1963. Corporate tax rates were also roughly twice what they are now. In Europe, things moved even farther in this direction. Britain, for example, established its National Health Service in 1948, and imposed substantially higher tax rates than the US, even during the tax-cutting regime of Margaret Thatcher. Without going into book-length specifics, we can note that there was a general trend in the first or "free" world during the 1950s and 60s toward high tax rates, robust public spending and relatively widely-shared prosperity. Poverty was not eradicated (and the benefits of general prosperity were often denied to African Americans and other minorities) but there was, at any rate, a large and growing middle class, an influential cohort that expected things to keep getting better, especially for their children.

Yet, starting in the 1970s, that progress eroded—until now we see rates of income and wealth-disparity that rival those of the 1890s. Many commentators are now saying that Polyani's views have been vindicated by the increasingly harsh and severe character of modern capitalism: debt burdens, austerity, huge and deepening inequality and the subjugation of national policies to global financial forces. But there are two ways of looking at those dire problems. Are we seeing the chickens of capitalism coming home to roost? Or, are we seeing the unsustainability of the very social-democratic, welfare-state policies that Polanyi advocated?

As economic factors or components, labor, money and land are quite different. What they have in common, according to Polanyi, is that they are too important to be commodified—their value must not be determined by self-interested market actors. If they are, their *social* value will be ignored, and society will fall into dysfunction. But there are, of course, huge questions of how these things would be valued, if not by the "higgling of the market." Let's look at each in turn.

Labor

People agree to work for employers, for a negotiated wage that is, by definition, less than the value of the goods and services that their labor-time creates. Were this not so, profit-seeking employers would not hire workers. For Marxists, this is the basis of surplus value, an inherent part of capitalist production. Thus, they believe that the "capitalist mode" inexorably leads to ever-worsening conditions for industrial workers and eventual revolution. The fact of surplus value is countermanded, however, (to a greater or lesser extent, depending on social conditions) by the fact that workers benefit from exchanging their labor-time for a given wage rate; doing so tends to get them a better return for their labor than their best alternative. This could be due to the economies of scale and other synergistic processes in a modern, interdependent economy (I might know how to do heart surgery, but not have my own hospital in which to perform it). But, it may also be due to an utter lack of alternatives for self-employment. In that case, employees still make a rational choice to accept the offered wage—it's better than the alternative: unemployment, and possibly starvation.

Georgists counter that commodification of labor is not the problem. Rather, it is the unjust and artificial restriction of labor's alternatives, caused in the main by land speculation, that increases the available supply of labor and lowers wages. The solution to this is to create a new economic situation in which unused and underused resources are put into production, thus providing those marginal workers with better alternatives. Because there is far more valuable land available than is currently being productively used, we can confidently predict that a Georgist economy would release usable rent-free land at the margin. In addition, because such land is currently in use and provided with public infrastructure, this existing infrastructure could be maintained, serving the newly-free land, at minimal cost to society. In such an economy, basic labor would have

realistic alternatives for self-employment, and wages would rise, as employers were obliged to compete for newly-scarce workers. Nevertheless, wages would still be set by market forces. The Georgist remedy would significantly raise their market value of workers, despite the fact that they would still be "commodified."

In an advanced Georgist economy, another policy alternative would be a basic income, paid to every citizen out of society's rent fund. This would further decrease the available supply of workers at a given wage level—without altering the basic fact that labor's return would be set by market forces.

Money

The colloquial sense of "commodity" is of a consumable item, produced for sale in the market. Money isn't that, obviously; it's a medium of exchange. Nevertheless, money is all about arms-length transactions, and one might think that if there's anything we shouldn't worry about being "commodified," it would be money. The issue for Polanyi was the danger of allowing market forces to determine the value, and therefore the supply, of money. He felt that would lead to panics, runs on banks, booms and busts, financial crises—and well, he seems to have been prescient on that score.

Economic historians point out that the institution of money

Key Facts About Money and Banking Today

The collateral for real estate loans is most often the real estate that the borrowed money is buying. This makes up more than 80% of the collateral base for loans today.

This tends to create speculative bubbles, in a self-reinforcing cycle. Land values are expected to rise. The collateral for the money people borrow to buy land is based on the value of the land, which includes a speculative premium. If the value of the collateral increases, more money can be borrowed—and if more borrowed money is available to buy land, the demand for land goes up, which tends to increase its price, which tends to increase its collateral value...!

But, of course, it can't go up forever. We ought to know; in the run-up to the Great Crash of 2008, society tried its very hardest to keep it going up forever. Local banks have reached their limit of new mortgage loans? No problem, big banks will take them off your hands for cash (as will the quasi-governmental organizations Fannie Mae and Freddie Mac, which acted like investment banks in this case). Banks will then bundle all these mortgage loans—shady ones and sound ones, all together—into mortgage-backed securities. This would allow banks to keep right on lending. But there are only so many credit-worthy borrowers? Not a problem—just extend subprime loans to people who are poorer credit risks. The financial structure gets more rickety. Eventually the camel's back is so loaded that it can't take even one more piece of straw.

was subsequent to, and evolved out of, credit—deferred exchanges based on trust within a community.[3] Yet over time, as horizons broadened, it became advantageous to have a means by which to confidently trade with strangers: thus the development of money, whose value people trust implicitly. Money is, essentially, a labor-saving invention, one of society's many "improvements in the arts of production."

In the 19th century, free trade policies coupled with adherence to the gold standard made it difficult for governments to intervene to help struggling workers in times of inflation or depression. Polanyi felt that the emphasis on "sound money" would always lead to the kind of social stress that gave rise to fascism in 20th-century Europe. Eventually, the gold standard gave way to the discipline of bond markets, which serve to further restrict governments' options to spend on social needs. Austerity has become a byword of the global economy.

Today, the supply of money is mainly determined by private credit markets; money is loaned into existence by banks. Central banks can influence the money supply by changing the base rate of interest, or altering banks' reserve requirements. However, they cannot determine the supply of money; uncontrolled spirals of either inflation or deflation are still possible. Some monetary reformers argue that the current system gives monopoly power to private banks, and that this is a terrible way to provide society with the money it needs. They argue that a better way would be for money not to be loaned into existence, but spent into existence by government. In the words of monetary reformer Stephen Zarlenga, money's fundamental nature is that of "an abstract legal power of government" whose control must be wrested from private hands.

Among the various theories about how things ought to be

divided up between individuals and the community, one sensible one is Henry George's contention that enterprises that are monopolies in their nature should be controlled by the government. Land ownership is a natural monopoly, of course. Others include railroad rights-of-way, highways, power lines, broadcast frequencies and sites in geosynchronous orbit.[4] How about banking? Undoubtedly there are many problems with money and banking today (for a rundown, just listen to any speech by Elizabeth Warren). But is private banking inherently monopolistic? If we give it a moment's thought, I think we'll have to see that it isn't. If I want to use a piece of land, I am competing against all the other people who want to use the same piece of land. The owner can charge the highest price that any one of us is willing to pay to get access to that site. But, if I want to borrow money, a number of banks are competing for my business. There may be fewer than there used to be, and they all might benefit from subsidies and guarantees that limit competition. But, if those cushions were taken away, the banking industry would be more competitive, not less. The basic problem isn't that the banking system is private—it's that privately-owned land is the major source of loan collateral.

Land

Our readers don't need to be reminded that private ownership of land is problematic. But, does that mean that land must not be commodified? There is a market in land; there long has been. Reports on this market make up a big part of the economic news. Land reform through public seizure and redistribution has never been a thinkable policy in developed economies, and in any case has never been effective. Here again, Henry George offers a sensible guiding principle. "It is not necessary to confiscate land," he wrote, "it is only necessary to confiscate rent." But rent is a market-based figure. You might even say that rent is the empirical result of a process of commodification.

One of the classic lines of criticism leveled at the Georgist remedy is the notion that by forcing land into use, it would lead to overdevelopment; society would build too high, eat up too much green space, use too much energy and spew too much pollution. This would fit with a glib reading of Polanyi's thesis: we can't just let *the market*—even a Georgist market—have its way with Mother Earth; we'll destroy her before we've even stopped to think. The fallacy in this is that it depends on an incorrectly restricted definition of "land." Obviously, local overdevelopment creates externalities. It is vital to remember the classic definition of *economic land*: "the entire material universe, except for human beings and their products." That includes the oceans and the atmospheric commons. Economic actors must be obliged to pay for *all* of the natural opportunities they use—and were they so obliged, prosperity would not bring an unsustainable environmental downside in its wake.

I would argue that this economic paradigm shift can happen, on the scale that it truly needs to happen, only if market forces are brought to bear. Consider the value of ecosystem services, which I believe is a resource rent like any other, and whose value therefore must serve as public revenue. It seems to me that local ecosystem services are quite accurately valued by the market, and their integration into conventional markets has had positive environmental impacts. We worry, rightly, about unsustainable overfishing in the oceans—yet fishing in inland rivers and lakes is effectively managed by government permitting. Collectively, private landowners, engaging in "NIMBY environmentalism," have helped to restore wildlife habitat with surprising speed in many parts of the United States. It won't be easy to impose market values on global ecosystem services—but it is by no means impossible.[5]

Damaging practices create costs that people actually pay. Assessing those costs is something that needs to be done, and smart people are working on ways to do it. I can't imagine how their value could possibly be recovered, if such things were considered off limits to the market.

Does the reader suspect this position to be insufficiently radical, or to represent a capitulation to right-wing or "capitalistic" sensibilities? If so, please be reminded that the atmospheric commons, which most people agree is under threat, is a global resource. Its protection depends on some form of global jurisdiction. The external costs of greenhouse-gas pollution are paid by the entire world. Indeed, I think this fact explains the seeming irrationality of climate-change deniers: to committed nationalists, global climate change is, literally, unthinkable. No doubt the task before us is dauntingly huge—but what's the alternative?

Sacred Land

Over the last couple of months the world has been watching the standoff over the Dakota Access Pipeline. The Sacred Stone Camp[6] now hosts a larger coalition of Native American groups than has gathered together in many decades. The proposed pipeline route doesn't explicitly cross the Standing Rock Sioux Reservation, but it does cross a number of ancient village and burial sites—as well as the Missouri River, which, in itself, makes a lot of people nervous.

Are they trying to build the pipeline across sacred land, and should it be opposed on that basis? That's a tough one: I mean, here I am arguing that we should marketize everything, in the name of economic justice! What about the market value of the sacred?

It may well be that things are so mixed up in our post-modern, post-industrial, post-everything world that a clear first-principled answer isn't always available. But let's see what we can do. I'd be the first to agree that separation of Church and State is an important principle, and justice is served by taking certain places out of economic consideration on that basis. I'd also agree that all Native Americans, and particularly the Sioux in this region, have been so egregiously robbed of their sovereign lands for so long that they deserve the benefit of the doubt in situations like this. And it could also be said that the cause of these gathered "Protectors"[7] has struck a chord in many people because of a deepening conviction that fossil fuel development has gone too far, that our biosphere is in peril and a stand ought to be taken. For all these reasons, I unequivocally support those who've gathered to protect Sioux lands against violation by an oil pipeline.

But that leaves open the larger question: what about *sacred* land? I always think of how Chief Seattle put it, when he was asked, by President Franklin Pierce, to sell his people's land. Seattle acknowledged that there was nothing he could do to stop this "sale" from going forward—yet it was, nevertheless, an utterly absurd and immoral concept. Seattle replied, "We will consider your offer. When we have decided, we will let you know. Should we accept, I here and now make this condition: we will never be denied to visit, at any time, the graves of our fathers and our friends." And where are these graves to be found? Seattle was clear: every square foot of every bit of land of the Americas.

We live in a modern, diversified, commodified economy—which, by the way, yields amazing benefits, enabling an undreamed-of level of prosperity, an astounding capacity for fulfilling the subtlest, most challenging human desires and aspirations. Yet, the inescapable truth of Seattle's speech, and of a great many indigenous traditions around the world, is that *all* land is sacred—including the air, the water, and everything under the ground. Nor is that an archaic notion; sacredness doesn't expire. I believe there is only one way we can resolve this paradox, and the time to do so is short. We should believe in the market; let it do its job and work its wonders—and we should make sure the community takes the market value of the earth for the benefit of all. That is the only way to make sure that all "commodities" will be truly and honorably valued.

~ *Georgist Journal* #129
October, 2016

End Notes

1. When that happens, it's only too likely that the idea's dogged advocates will get no credit. History will bestow its praise on whichever politicians happen to be in office at the time, but that's the way it goes.

2. Two readable recent articles on Polanyi: "Karl Polanyi Explains It All" by Robert Kuttner, and "Why Karl Polanyi Still Matters" by David Bollier.

3. For example, Henry George wrote in *The Science of Political Economy*, "Trust or credit is indeed the first of all the instrumentalities that facilitate exchange. Its use antedates not merely the use of any true money, but must have been coeval with the first appearance of man."

4. such orbital sites are unique by definition, and of great value for their uses in communications, GPS or reconnaissance.

5. For example, see Plassman and Tideman, "Accurate Valuation in the Absence of Markets."

6. Look it up on Google maps, just outside of Cannon Ball, North Dakota

7. They call themselves this, highlighting the media's characterization of them as "protesters."

— Chapter 16 —

Getting It Together
in Bangladesh

Bangladesh has been in the news lately, mainly because of the Rohingya refugees that have been pouring into it from Myanmar—close to a million of them. We can be pretty sure that the treatment of the Rohingya in Myanmar has been very bad—if for no other reason than the fact of where they've been going; Bangladesh has nothing close to sumptuous accommodations for them.

I had been wondering about conditions in Bangladesh, because of its geographic status as a place certain to get hit very hard indeed by the forces of climate change. It is low-lying, full of rivers and deltas which are being massively swelled by accelerating glacier melt from the Himalayas. Additionally, India diverts large amounts of water to irrigation during growing seasons—and then releases it Bangladesh's way during rainy ones, exacerbating flooding. If you can think of any one nation that would be getting slammed by climate change, Bangladesh would be the one.

And yet, a bit of cursory Googling reveals heartening surprises about how things are going these days in Bangladesh. Despite the many geographic, demographic and geopolitical challenges this nation faces, in a number of key measures, it is doing much better than nations that seem to face far fewer challenges. Bangladesh's economy grew by 7.1% in 2016, and it grew by at least 6% for each of the previous six years. Its middle class is expanding much more quickly than comparable developing nations—it is said to be closing in on the "middle range" societies, those that are developing an appreciably influential middle class. Life expectancies and infant-mortality numbers have improved significantly. It cannot be doubted that there's some good stuff going on in Bangladesh.

A *Scientific American* article about the horrific effects of climate change in Bangladesh nevertheless offered these facts:

> *Fazle Karim Chowdhury, a Member of Parliament, who explained, with a measure of pride, "once there was a shortage of food; now we export food." Bangladesh once led the world in child mortality. No longer. Due to better health care, life expectancy rose from 59 to 69 between 1990 and 2010. Providing free birth control empowered women and reduced the fertility rate from seven children per woman to three, which is substantially lowering population growth rates. Universal primary education is helping to create a more skilled workforce. Perhaps most impressive, the poverty rate declined from 57 percent to 25 percent between 1990 and 2014.*

A widely-publicized terror attack 2016 hit the popular Holey Artisan Bakery in the capital city of Dhaka—and some suicide bombings followed. However, these had been the first Islamist terror attacks in Bangladesh since before 2005. On balance, Bangladesh has seen very little terrorist activity. ISIS has declared a desire to open up some form of "Islamic State" front in Bangladesh, due to its strategic location—but, there seems to be little indication that such efforts are gaining traction.

The Big News: The Rohingya

As has been widely reported, the Rohingya Muslims of Myanmar have been fleeing unspeakably horrible conditions of ethnic cleansing, and the vast majority of them have gone to the closest place they could reach, across the border from Myanmar's Rakhine

State, to the Cox's Bazaar region in Bangladesh. Nearly 1,000,000 of them have settled in makeshift refugee camps in Cox's Bazaar. Seven other Muslim countries have absorbed about 750,000 Rohingya refugees. Ill-equipped Bangladesh has borne the greatest burden, by far. A group of NGOs and foundations have announced a goal to raise $434 million to aid the Rohingya; it's not yet clear how much of that will be delivered.

There are some indications that this massive influx of suffering and needy refugees has engendered some political controversy in Bangladesh. There are some reports of "increased authoritarian tendencies," but in general, the political upshot of this seems to be rather slight. Indications are that Bangladesh is simply doing its best to make do in a difficult situation, providing what meager sanitation, water and food supplies they can in the gigantic Cox's Bazaar refugee camps. Though it may seem callous to say so, one gets the impression that Bangladesh's Rohingya situation is just one more thing on the list of difficult challenges that the country is dealing with. Last fall, a proposal was floated in the parliament to relocate a couple of hundred thousand of the Rohingya to a small, entirely inadequate and indeed sinking island in the Bay of Bengal—but fortunately the proposal seems to have been shelved.

Dhaka: the Megacity's Megacity

Bangladesh's capital city, Dhaka, is by all accounts an astoundingly busy place. Its current population is estimated at 18 million, and it is growing by some 400,000 people every year. It is the world's fastest-growing city. The incentives for such explosive growth aren't hard to identify: things like the stresses to the countryside caused by sea-level rise, severe cyclones and those melting Himalayan glaciers. And, as chaotic as the capital city might seem, it promises attractive economic opportunities, compared to the profound stresses faced by subsistence farmers (despite the fact that Bangladesh's delta-enriched soils have traditionally been some of the most fertile in the entire world). There are old sections of Dhaka that boast architectural treasures, but, of course, huge tracts

of the city now amount to little more than shanty-towns, informal settlements such as are seen in any number of developing-country megacities. Yet one gets the distinct impression that in Dhaka, all of these processes are intensified—not just those that lead to chaos, but also those that lead to prosperity. Still, like most of Bangladesh, Dhaka is quite close to sea level. Surrounded by great rivers whose flows have become increasingly unpredictable in recent years, Dhaka is estimated to be the worst-situated urban area in the world. Flooding is endemic. Local transportation is often provided by rickshaw drivers, who can frequently be seen pedaling through streets with two feet of water in them. These guys have to have the strongest quadriceps in all of Asia!

And yet, somehow, most of those hordes of people pouring into Dhaka are managing to make a living. Dhaka is by no means a wealthy city; average family income there is currently about $170 per month—but that is up. A recent World Bank report showed that income for the poorest 40% of Bangladeshis grew by half a percentage point during that period during the last six years of strong growth; in India, that trend was precisely the reverse. Yale economist Ahmed Mushfiq, quoted in Quartz Media, said, "Bangladesh's recent success can be attributed to two major factors: the flourishing garment manufacturing industry and the country's robust NGO sector."

What we mostly recall in the West about the Bangladeshi garment industry is the horrible 2013 collapse of the eight-story Rana Plaza building outside Dhaka, in which 1,100 workers were killed. It would be an exaggeration to say that working conditions in Bangladesh's garment industry have been transformed; the labor market is still very competitive—but the profits to be gained in the industry have created incentives for far more hospitable working conditions. Today's factories tend to be clean and efficiently run. In 2015 Bangladesh exported over $26 billion worth of clothing, second only to China.

Demographics have played a fortuitous role as well. Eighty percent of workers in the garment industry are women, and it is clear that economic empowerment of women tends to have an outsized influence on economic development generally. Among Muslim countries, Bangladesh has long enjoyed a reputation for religious tolerance. There has been some unrest and inter-religious violence in recent years—but far less than has been seen in, say, Pakistan. Most encouragingly, economic and health indicators for women in Bangladesh have improved across the board since the early 2000s. The broader demographic picture is favorable as well: unlike many developing countries, some 40% of Bangladesh's population is now in its most-productive age range: 25-54 years.

In a country starting from as low an economic level as Bangladesh has, what these trends lead to is the rise of a middle class. "Middle-class" can be defined in various ways. Business interests looking for marketing opportunities in Bangladesh seem to be defining it as a household income of $5,000 a year or more, a level of income that tends to allow Bangladeshis to buy "luxury items" such as air-conditioners, refrigerators, or automobiles—all of which are beginning to sell well in Bangladesh.

Meanwhile, in Dhaka

It certainly stands to reason that the lion's share of economic growth and activity in Bangladesh would be taking place in the capital city. That's where everyone is going; that's where things are happening. Yet that is where the chaos is greatest! Many commentators have reported that Dhaka's most defining characteristic is its horrendously snarled, essentially immobile transportation situation. It takes literally hours to get anywhere in this city. A relatively small

number of automobiles have recently appeared in the city; they confer prestige and status, but the streets are by no means designed for them, and they take up a lot of room. In fact, people try to get around Dhaka in every imaginable kind of conveyance, from rickshaws and donkey carts, to the small three-wheeled motorized taxicabs that are quite common, to bicycles and feet—all trying to make their way through the same narrow and frequently-flooded streets. Indeed, the rivers of Dhaka are nearly as crowded as the streets; watercraft of all sizes (and degrees of repair) careen dangerously around the city on the rivers. The entire transport picture in Dhaka is one of nearly-incomprehensible randomness and chaos. It's very hard to imagine how goods get to market, how business people get to appointments or how children get to school.

The Khan Mohammad Mridha Mosque, Old Dhaka

A great deal could be done to improve the flow of traffic in Dhaka. It would take careful study, of course—and any solution would have to account for all of the local, organic factors of Dhaka's unique traffic situation. Simply dedicating certain pathways to each of the many different kinds of conveyances that are now poured onto Dhaka's zany streets would be a tremendous improvement. If the tricycle taxis, for example, didn't have to dodge the rickshaws and the donkey carts, they could vastly decrease their travel times. If I could suggest a policy, I would ask a consortium of well-placed foundations, such as the Gates, the Clinton, the MacArthur, etc., to pull together a fund of $300 million to design and implement a comprehensive traffic flow plan for the city of Dhaka. This plan could not simply come from outside experts. It would have to be designed, from the ground up, with input from the people who actually live in and try to travel in Dhaka. Such a well-funded plan would probably even have some money left over to start creating some of the necessary infrastructure. Yet the initial plan's goal would not be to build a lot of superhighways, but rather to come up with a comprehensive plan that would help Dhaka make the most efficient use of its existing roads, streets and waterways. Of course, new transportation infrastructure—including public transportation systems—would be forthcoming. But that calls for more funding. Let's talk about that in a moment.

It might be reasonable to expect the United States government to contribute some of this exploratory funding. One might think the US would benefit in terms of goodwill as well as business—but that's not going to happen. Our current administration simply thinks that "those Muslims" want "our jobs." Our current administration is in fact quite stupid about this. You can get a perfectly-good pair of Bangladesh-made jeans at Walmart for twenty bucks. But have you priced a pair of 100% American-made Levi's jeans lately? Their most popular pair, model 501, original fit, will run you $168. Other US-made Levi's jeans can be had for as little as $88. Sometimes shipping is free.

We Have A Few Modest Proposals

As Georgists, we pay a lot of attention to the issue of public revenue; we don't seem to be able to avoid it. But, it's not merely an obsession; we believe that society's choices about public revenue reveal the most important aspects of the essential relationship between individuals and the community. The leading source of tax revenue in Bangladesh is the value-added tax, or VAT, at just under 30% of overall revenue. The next-largest sources are import duties and personal and corporate income taxes—which take relatively smaller bites. From a business-competitiveness point of view, the news is somewhat good; Bangladesh's ratio of tax rate to GDP is considerably lower than India's. Nevertheless, the VAT is by no means an efficient or advantageous source of public revenue. It is sometimes defended on the grounds of encouraging exports—particularly, if the country exports a lot to the United States, which (luckily for us) has no VAT. But that is hardly a good reason to have a VAT, if there is any better alternative.

Well, there is. A landmark 2010 study, done by Ahsan H. Mansur and Mohammad Yunus for the Policy Research Institute of Bangladesh, detailed the many inefficiencies of the VAT in Bangladesh, and recommended replacing it with the system of broad-based capital gains and land value taxes.

We recommend land value taxation—most particularly in crowded, growing cities. A place like Dhaka probably has many lingering land-tenure and cadastral issues. Yet these problems are unlikely to be intractable. The city certainly has a functioning and indeed lively real estate market. Given the extreme density of population—and therefore the intense level of involvement of Dhaka's people with literally every square inch of the ground they occupy, it stands to reason that the people have a very clear seat-of-the-pants understanding of what Dhaka real estate is worth. Under such conditions, a highly-accurate land cadaster would require just two things: a sincere desire among its organizers to find and publish accurate data, and real input from normal people. These aren't sure things politically, of course, but they are at least conceivable.

Various accounts show real estate values in Dhaka as having risen

by about 90% over the past ten years. It seems that some cautious optimism would be justified about the positive effects of $300 million being spent on designing and implementing improved traffic patterns. How could that not bump up land values in Dhaka?

So: here are my modest proposals. I don't claim to have any particular political sway over the situation, obviously—I'll just submit that they make enough sense to merit real consideration. First, Bangladesh should scrap the VAT. Just do away with it; it never was any good. The roughly 29% of national revenue it now provides could be made up with land value taxes over a three-or-four-year phase-in period. In fairly short order, buildings, commerce and even personal income could be made exempt from taxation. Would that not accelerate all of the positive economic trends in Bangladesh, and even, possibly provide funding to help abate some of the most dangerous threats posed by climate change?

It does not do to try to minimize or gloss over the exceedingly daunting problems faced by developing megacities such as Dhaka. Yet at the same time, it has been well-established that the overall ecological footprint, the economic efficiency and the per-capita sustainability of production improves when poor people move from stressed, impoverished rural areas into cities. With all of Dhaka's urban stresses, those processes are manifestly going on there, right now. With some sensible city-planning and public revenue policies, this "world's most chaotic city" could become a great 21st-century success story.

- Earthsharing.org
2018

— Chapter 17 —

A Moral Structure to Address Climate Change

Harrison Moore, Unsplash, harrison-moore-apbQ77SBWiE-unsplash.jpg

It seems to us that the climate-change issue should have a moral aspect to it. After all, we're messing up our world. We're helping well-connected resource-grabbers to exploit poor people and vulnerable natural habitats. We feel that it shouldn't go on this way. The world is losing hundreds and hundreds of species. Innocent island nations are disappearing without a trace. Floods and storms and fires are unleashed on the undeserving, while the well-to-do shelter behind high-quality insurance and well-provisioned rescue departments.

Yes, it seems like it ought to be fairer, but how can we make it so without destroying the Western economy? We wring our hands over carbon-tax proposals, none of which seems even remotely sufficient. When it comes right down to it, aren't we caught up in a perception that things have gone too far; they're out of control, the most drastic steps we can take won't be enough, it's too late for sensible policy proposals!

Simple fairness seems a quaint idea at a time like this. Too many entrenched systems vying for dominance.

Yet doesn't there have to be some guiding element of fairness to it? Otherwise aren't we just banging around in chaos?

In 1879, Henry George was the first person in English to write about a "spaceship earth," in *Progress and Poverty*: "It is a well-provisioned ship, this on which we sail through space."

Some would accuse George of quickly turning this cosmic observation into a prosaic one: "If the bread and beef above decks seem to grow scarce, we but open a hatch and there is a new supply, of which before we never dreamed. And very great command over the services of others comes to those who as the hatches are opened are permitted to say, 'This is mine!'" But I don't think George was saying the ship just had so many supplies, all of which were owned by the captain and his friends. A ship on the sea has various ways of finding food and water, and getting to port, more easily done if they share their supplies rather than fight over them. A well-provisioned ship isn't infinitely provisioned.

There is a moral framework that applies to climate-change policy. It is symmetrical and comprehensive—but it has just one drawback: it may be seen as impracticably unfeasible. But it can't be. If it is, we're, screwed.

I'm referring to the moral basis of ownership described by Henry George in *Progress and Poverty*. This is a basic, organic, conception of things. It says that the value of natural resources and opportunities, land sites, everything provided by nature, belongs to the community. And there's one other big part of it. Any harm caused by some "productive" effort—such as, say, a plastics manufacturing plant just off of New York's East River, which spews fumes into the air and wildlife-killing effluvia into the water, owes the community the full cost incurred by that pollution. Chances are, if those costs were part of doing business, such a plant would not locate there in the first place (or it wouldn't be that sort of plant).

It has always been a strong feature of "the Georgist Remedy" or "the Single Tax Solution" that it can be implemented effectively at a municipal level. It would be good if whole societies would do it, but cities can get started just fine, and reap most of the benefits. What benefits? Efficient use of space and infrastructure. Infill development. Use-appropriate development. The list goes on; talk to the good folks at www.urbantools.org.

But for our moral climate-change strategy, some major city would have to go all in—no namby-pamby gradualism. The people of, say, New York would have to go ahead and shove their site values into the abyss of efficiency and justice. Other cities would have little choice but to follow suit. We'd soon see how well that works Then, we could get started on the national programs.

If we approach the climate-change issue with the comprehensive strategy that resource rents belong to the community in every single case, then we have the potential to implement a self-balancing, self-reinforcing set of solutions. We can have trade-ons, not trade-offs.

Here are a few policy implications:

Fossil Fuels—natural resources (fuel in the ground) and locations belong to the community; user must pay for access—may sell energy once created but must pay to mitigate harm (this cost would be passed on to consumers, and will probably make coal and oil impracticable). Unlike common carbon-tax proposals, the Georgist plan would seek to recover the full harm caused by burning the fossil fuel. We hope this would be offset by the other robust incentives our program would create. Suppose we go ahead and make coal and oil unfeasible in 2-3 years' time, and see how quickly we can replace them with renewables and distributed local sources? Remember that some 80% of today's greenhouse-gas emissions come from fossil fuels. Getting rid of them is the ball game; and our proposal offers widespread synergies. How long would we have to wear sweaters?

Renewables—location belongs to the community; user pays for access, may sell energy once created but must pay to mitigate harm. Wind or solar locations are often fairly marginal. There would be a big construction push. Cost-effectiveness with fossil-fuel sources is approaching, and with economies of scale, it would be realized.

Nuclear—natural resource (fuel in the ground) and location belong to community; producer may sell energy but must pay to safely dispose of waste. Incentives for nuclear power would be very low, maybe just enough to gradually decommission existing plants.

Distributed *(local)* **Energy Sources**—user pays for location, may sell surplus energy back to grid; must pay to mitigate harm, if any. Possible discounts/rebates if this use reduces costs of grid energy. Lots of incentive to develop & market new forms of these.

Urban—obviously, full site value belongs to community, and zero tax on buildings. On-site energy production (as in tall buildings) can be discounted against site value charge to incentivize green development. Surplus goods or energy can be sold.

Agricultural—site value belongs to community. Crop belongs to producer, who must pay to mitigate harm, including that of meat, especially beef; site value should be computed to reflect sustainable, labor-intensive uses that minimize negative externalities.

Mixed Uses—such as energy/agricultural; urban/energy—site rent can be adjusted accordingly.

Infrastructure—full public collection of site rents would create incentives for infill/replacement. New sprawl developments should be discouraged in short term, possibly via zoning.

Forests/Oceans—their carbon sequestration value should be estimated. This could form the basis for a fair payment toward climate change adaptation.

Shipping—this should be singled out for special consideration. Black soot should be outlawed if possible. Feedback effects in the Arctic need to be addressed internationally. Will this affect the economies of global trade? Probably, but it could help to stimulate local, labor-intensive production.

Permafrost—this will serve as a barometer for overall greenhouse-gas reduction. If it keeps melting too quickly, we need to do better.

Climate Change Adaptation—the situation has become dire enough that mere tax incentives won't get us all the way there. In some areas, especially when multiple nations are affected, treaty-driven command-and-control methods will be needed, and richer nations will have to invest more.

This will decrease site values in many places: the need for sea walls, flood protection, fire/storm protection, etc. It will demand federal resources! Some countries have such resources available—like the US with its huge military budget. Others will have to share; the UN will need to play a role. "Defense" will need to shift from national conflict to climate defense. US military is already planning for this sort of thing. Resources exist; China is able to build military islands in the South China Sea. But unlike fighter jets, this will be an investment in a sustainable future.

No other proposed strategy for climate change offers the sort of synergy and balance that this plan does. We shouldn't be persuaded by those who insist that "it's more complicated than that." It really is not. Make sure resource rents belong 100% to the community, and everything falls into place!

So far, most people have been either too busy, too fearful—or too well-served by the status quo—to stop and think about the truth of those words. But they will. Eventually it will dawn on them that nothing else will work.

~ Progress.org
April, 2019

Adapted from the script of the final segment in a new 16-part video series sponsored by the Henry George School and narrated by the author.

Lindy Davies
(1957-2019)

Lindrith Davies of Jackson, Maine, died on April 9, 2019, after a 15-month illness with esophageal cancer that had metastasized to his brain. He leaves his wife, Lisa Cooley, and his children, Eli Morris and Francesca June. He is also survived by his father, Morris Davies of Georgetown, Maryland and Austin, Texas, and sisters Cristina Davies of Albuquerque, New Mexico, Heather Davies Bernard of Austin, Texas, and Jennifer Davies-Reazor of Newark, Delaware. His mother, Janet Davies, died in 2018. All his extended family and his friends are shocked and saddened by his loss; his intelligence, his humor, his wit and wisdom, his energy for work and play will be deeply missed by everyone who knew him.

A Quaker memorial service and celebration of Lindy's life took place on May 19th at 2:00 pm, at the Jackson Community Center, Jackson, Maine.

Lindy was born on October 9, 1957, and grew up in George-town, Maryland. He grew up along the shores of his beloved Sas-safras River, exploring its curves and twists, its muddy and tree-lined shores. His childhood was full of those solitary ramblings as well as his love of archery, rocketry, and as he grew to adolescence, writing. Lindy was ecstatic when eventually, Cristy, Jenny and Heather came along. He loved being a big brother.

He graduated from Kent County High in 1975 and went to Denison University in Ohio. He grew to love the little town of Granville, Ohio, and his proudest achievement in college was as producer and director of an off-campus production of a play by Ray Bradbury.

After college, Lindy worked in the family auto parts business for a few years, a period of footloose uncertainty that he wrote about in his novel, *The Sassafras Crossing*. He took the opportunity to work for a tree surgery crew in the mid-80s where he met Mike Curtis, a tree surgeon and advocate of the economic ideas of Henry George. This encounter grew into a friendship that changed his di-rection and his life. After a catastrophic fall from a tree in 1986, he quit the tree crew and returned to school for a masters in educa-tion. When George Collins, director of the Philadelphia Henry George School took the position of director of the New York school, Lindy went with him as assistant director.

Lindy loved living in New York. He joined the Brooklyn Society of Friends, and became a denizen of the Village Gate's weekly open-mike jazz sessions. This brought him to another lifelong friend, Village Gate bartender, Ms Sonny Rivera. In January of 1994, the Village Gate closed for good; in February, he joined Echo, a small New York-based online community, where he met Lisa Cooley, the love of his life. He joined her as she sat on the floor in front of the fireplace at the Art Bar at one of Echo's weekly gath-erings; he always said he felt as though he had to give up one love—the Village Gate—so he could find Lisa. They married at Brooklyn Friends in March of 1995 and were happy for the 25 years they were together.

Eli was born in 1997 and Francie in 2000. He was hopelessly dedicated to his children. Not making enough money to live comfortably in NYC, knowing that they would have to put the kids in daycare at 6 weeks old, they took Lisa's parents up on the offer of a house site on their land in central Maine, pulled up stakes and moved north when Eli was 3 months old.

The *Henry George Institute*, a non-profit that was in Lindy's care since the death of its founder, Bob Clancy, in 1994, moved to Maine with the family, and Lindy spent the next 22 years building it as an educational organization committed to teaching political economy to "regular people." Lindy was a worker. He built his family a house, managed the Institute, and cared for Lisa and his kids. He was in constant motion, moving from one project to the next with energy. Very ambitious for the Institute, he produced the quarterly *Georgist Journal*, administered the worldwide correspondence lessons, created online courses, and maintained multiple websites dedicated to Henry George. He became involved in studying the property tax policies of New York City and spent countless hours poring over its assessment database.

At the same time, he maintained the house he built for his family, helped care for Lisa's aging parents, spent time with his kids, and was the best husband anyone has ever seen.

When Eli was seven, he and Lindy started fencing with the Downeast School of Fencing. This became a beloved pastime for both of them. Lindy was a proud papa when his son started, in his own words, "wiping the floor with his old man." They fenced together for many years. He also accompanied Francie to violin lessons, dance classes (he wrote *The Sassafras Crossing* in Cappy's Chowder House in Camden waiting for Francie to finish rehearsals) and recitals. His kids constantly amazed and delighted him.

About 6 years ago he started work on a novel, which he finished 2 years later. *The Sassafras Crossing* is available on Amazon! He loved writing fiction and poetry, and a big regret of his life was not having time enough to dedicate to it. Had the cancer not happened, he would have dedicated part of his time to new ideas, as he and Lisa grew into their senior years side-by-side; Lisa working on plays, Lindy on fiction. (The next novel was to be a murder mystery set in a fictional version of the Village Gate.) But that's not what fate had in store for them.

Lindy was constantly doing, and his life was cut short when he had so much left to do.

In his last months, Lindy's only desire, besides seeing Lisa and the kids well cared-for, was seeing that the Institute would survive him. There is now a team of dedicated friends and Georgists working on carrying this work forward. Anyone who would like to see that Lindy's life's work continues can send donations to:

Henry George Institute
4075 Cheltonham Court
Plainfield, Indiana 46168 USA

Lindy was the heart and soul of The *Henry George Institute*. The HGI board is determined to carry on the work that Lindy did as its Program Director. You can reach them at:

HenryGeorgeInstitute@gmail.com

HGI's websites, all created by Lindy, include:

http://www.henrygeorge.org
http://landreform.org/bob/
http://truefreetrade.org/
http://politicaleconomy.org/
http://www.georgistjournal.org/
http://www.masongaffneyreader.com/
http://prosperidad.org/

Lindy updated many of these to be mobile-friendly.
In 2012, Lindy successfully sought college credit recommendation for the 3-course series, which renewed in 2017.

Books Lindy published under HGI's banner include:

Understanding Economics: To Fix What's Wrong (2018)

Rent as Public Revenue: Issues and Methods (2018)

The Mason Gaffney Reader: Essays on Solving the "Unsolvable" (2013) (See Lindy's introduction at: http://www.masongaffneyreader.com/

The Alodia Scrapbook: Creating a New Paradigm (2010)

The Georgist Journal, at http://www.georgistjournal.org/

Three study guides:
Understanding Economics
Applied Economics: Globalization and Trade
Economic Science

For RSF, Lindy abridged *The Science of Political Economy* and wrote the afterword, "What George 'Left Out'" (2015)

Lindy's writings can also be seen at:
https://www.progress.org/authors/lindy-davies

At the Council of Georgist Organizations meeting in Pittsburgh in July 2019, we remembered Lindy, who played a significant role in the CGO.

The Sassafras Crossing by Lindrith Davies
was published in 2016 (ISBN: 978-0592706183).
It is available from www.amazon.com

Index

Names & Subjects

Abolition of taxation – 7
Achenbaum, Wyn – 7, 8
Adams, Douglas - 64
Agriculture – 109
Akamai (internet tech company) –
  66, 69, 70
Applied Economics – 22
Aristotle
  On value, based on a commodity's
  utility – 24
Asset Bubbles
  Dot.com bubble – 65
  Lending on real estate as cause –
  90
Association and equality – 80
"Association in equality" – 7
Atmospheric pollution – 94
Austrian economists – 26-28
Bangladesh – 97-105
Banking – 89-92

Bible – 84
Brazil, land hoarding, consequences
  of – 12
Brooklyn Society of Friends – 112
Capitalism
  Profits under – 24-25
Carbon sequestration – 109
Carrying capacity – 11. 32
Chattel slavery
  Compared to private land
  ownership – 85
Cheney, Dick - 84
Chief Seattle – 78-79, 95
Civilization, decline of – 80
Clancy, Bob
  Artwork by – 85
  Death of – 113

Founding of Henry George
  Institute – 6
Class struggle
  Henry George on – 43-44
Cleveland, Polly – 8
Climate Change – 97
  As a moral issue – 106-110
Collins, George L. – 8, 112
Commodities
  Defined – 86
  Fictitious – 86-96
Commons
  Atmospheric – 94
  Internet as – 65
Cooley, Lisa – 8, 111-114
Corporations – 37-41, 87
Council of Georgist Organizations –
  8, 115
Credentials in Economics
  Not required for understanding
  fundamental economics – 15
Cults, elements of – 15
Curtis, Mike – 8, 112
  Introduction – 9-10
Das Kapital – 48
Davies, family members
  Cristina Davies – 111
  Eli Davies – 8, 111, 113
  Francesca Davies – 8, 111, 113
  Heather Davies Bernard – 111
  Janet Davies – 111
  Jennifer Davies-Reazon – 111
  Lisa Cooley – 8, 10, 111, 114
  Morris Davies – 111
Davies, Lindy – 6-8
  As interpreter of the Georgist
  paradigm – 7
  Biography – 9-10, 111-114
  Death of – 6, 111

On importance of teaching justice
– 8
deMille, Agnes George
Corporations, cartels and real
power – 36-37
Desires – 31
Satisfaction of – 55, 75
Diaz, Philippe – 34
Direct democracy
To decide legislative questions –
22
Distribution (of wealth and services)
– 76
Division of labor
And Marxist surplus value theory
- 25
Dodson, Ed – 8
Douglas, Roy
Why wars become possible – 19
Eastern Economic Association – 62
Economic growth – 75
Economic justice
Solution to world's problems – 16
Economics by Samuelson and
Nordhaus – 23
Ecosystem services – 62, 76, 93
Edge-server caching – 66-67
Education
Importance of teaching justice –
18-19
Elections
United States, need for reform -
21
Energy sources – 109
Environmentalism/ist – 78, 93
Equality and association
Versus private land ownership –
82
Ethiopia
Land Hoarding, consequences of
– 12
Externalities – 77
Factors of production

How services fit in – 30-33
Farino, Ernest – 8
Fascists/ism – 80, 91
Fencing
Downeast School of Fencing –
113
Feudalism
As transitional stage of land tenure
– 59-60
Foldvary, Fred
Privileges granted to enterprise –
40

Frontier, closing of the virtual –
63-71
Gaffney, Mason – 7, 9, 10
George, Henry – 9, 30, 31, 34, 35,
42-47, 59, 74, 80, 85, 107
Class struggle – 43-44
Faith in social science when based
on natural law - 28
Influence of – 7
Mayoral campaign of 1886 – 20
Meaning of true democratic
government – 22
On the labor theory of valaue –
52, 53
On the labor theory of property –
54
George, Henry, Jr.
Election to the U.S. House of
Representatives – 20
Natural monopolies and corporate
privilege - 40
Georgist
Defined – 7
Paradigm – 7
Principles – 7
Remedy – 107
Theory of History – 42-47
Georgist Journal – 6, 8, 10, 13, 16,
19, 29, 33, 35, 41, 47, 62, 70,
73, 77, 85, 96,   113, 114, 115

Georgist Movement
  Embracing being called a Georgist
    – 48-50
  Focus on ending land monopoly
    reconsidered – 86
  Minimal progress thereof – 14
  Modernizing the Georgist message
    – 36
  Options for future activism – 35
Gilded Age – 9
Giles, Richard – 34
Globalization
  And wasteful over-transportation
    of goods – 46
Great Crash of 2008 – 90

Gross Domestic Product (GDP)
  Correlation to quality of life - 57
  As flawed indicator of economic
    progress – 33
Guthrie, Woody - 80

Gwartney, Ted – 8
Henry George Institute (HGI) – 8,
  10, 113, 114, 115
  Founding by Bob Clancy – 6
Henry George School in New York –
  10
Herman, Gil – 8
History, theories of – 42-62
Housing (expensive) - 73
Hudson, Michael
  Henry George's analysis not a true
    doctrine – 49-50
Industrial Revolution - 55
Infrastructure – 87, 109
Interest rates – 72
International Union for Land Value
  Taxation and Free Trade (the IU)
  As co-publisher of the *Georgist
    Journal* – 6, 8
Internet – 63-71
  As a free public good – 63-65

Internet Freedom Preservation Act –
  71
Jackson, Maine
  Community Center – 111
Johnson, Tom L.
  Mayor of Cleveland, Ohio – 20
Justice – 7, 8
  And right to live and work on
    earth – 18
  Economic – 16, 36
Keynes, John Maynard - 83
Keynesians – 48
Knowledge and skill – 58-61
Labor – 7, 88, 89
Labor Theory of Value – 24, 25, 52,
  53
  Treated in The Science of Political
    Economy – 52-53
Lao Tzu
  Quoted on turning weakness into
    strength – 14
Land – 7, 9
  Arable – 12
  Defined - 74, 79
  Sacred – 94
  Source of socially-created wealth -
    9
  Value – 28
Land hoarding
  Consequences of – 12
  In New York City – 72
Land nationalization
  Resisted in developed economies –
    92
Land speculation
  Cause of lower wages - 88
Land Tenure
  Communal throughout most of
    history – 59
  Private ownership – 78-85
  Private ownership a natural
    monopoly – 92
Landlord's Game, The – 34

Lappé, Frances Moore – 34
Law of development as the law of
    integration – 44-45
Law of Rent is unrepealable – 41
Liberty – 7
Maine – 10, 111
Malthus, Thomas Robert - 82
Malthusians
    Neo- – 11, 12
Malthusian collapse – 76
Margin of production – 69, 89
Market Failure
    Caused by monopoly, subsidy or
    political manipulation – 26-27
Marx, Karl
    On concentration of wealth - 83
    On labor theory of value – 24-26
    On history – 44

Marxist Theory of History
    Based on historical materialism -
    43
Marxist Theory of Value – 24-26, 53
Marxists – 48, 49, 88
Médaille, John – 35
Megacity – 98
Menger, Carl
    Austrian theory of value – 26
Mill, John Stuart
    On the production and
    distribution of wealth – 51, 61
Minter, Vajramati – 8
Money – 89-92

Monopolies
    Subject to government control –
    92
Myanmar – 97, 98
Native Americans – 94, 95
Natural Laws of production and
    distribution of wealth – 51

Neoclassical economists – 49

Neo-Malthusians – 11, 12
Net Neutrality – 63, 67, 68, 69
New Deal – 87
New York City – 6, 10, 72, 73, 112
Nymoen, Rich – 8
Overdevelopment
    And the public collection of rent –
    92-93
Overpopulation – 11-13
Pakistan – 101

Peace, not simply the absence of
    armed conflict – 18
Permafrost – 110
Perry, Ted (screenwriter) – 78
Phillips, Lizzie Magie
    Creator of The Landlord's Game -
    34
Pierce, Franklin – 78, 95
Plassman (Florenz) – 96
Plato, on value as inherent in a
    commodity – 24
Polanyi, Karl
    Fictitious commodities – 86-88,
    93, 96
Political Economy
    Defined by Henry George – 51,
    74-77
    Defined in Henry George
    Institute material to include
    services - 74

Pollard, Harry
    Meaning of privilege to a Georgist
    – 23
Pollution
    Not a free good – 76
    Greenhouse-gas - 93
Population
    Causes of high birth rates - 12
    Density – 11
    Neo-Malthusian views on over-
    population – 11-13

Post, Louis F.
  Assistant Secretary of Labor – 20

Poverty
  Not caused by increases in
    population – 11-13
Privilege – 23
  Corporate form of – 36-41
Progress (human, social)
  Cause of decline – 80-81
  Enhanced by equality and
    association – 42, 80-82
  Law of development is the law of
    integration – 44-45
  States of defined - 60
Progress and Poverty – 7, 9, 14, 36,
  47, 54, 61, 62, 75, 80, 85, 107
Property, labor theory of – 54
Property in Land – see Land Tenure
Property Tax – 72
Proportional Representation
  Alternative to winner-take-all
    elections – 21-22
Quality of Life – 57
Rack Rent
  Defined – 53
Refugees – 97-98
  Rohingya Muslims of Myanmar –
    98-99
Real estate speculators – 73
Renewables – 108
Rent
  As applied to the internet – 69
  Coming from ecosystem services –
    76-77
  Confiscation by the community/
    society justified – 92
  Law of – 17, 41
Resource rents – 110
Ricardo, David
  On labor theory of value - 24, 53,
    61
Ricardians – 48

Rights
  To own land – 16
Rivera, Sonny – 112
Robert Schalkenbach Foundation
  (RSF) – 8, 10, 61, 115
  Film produced by Philippe Diaz –
    34
Sacred Land
  Development issues – 94-96
Sassafras River – 9
Selfishness, versus sympathy – 54
Services – 30-33, 62, 74, 75
  Defined by Henry George – 30
  How to address in classroom
    teaching of political economy –
    50-51
  Part of production - 59
  Role in the production and
    distribution of wealth – 30-33
Single Tax – 7
  Potential to implement at the local
    level – 107-108
  Solution to the land problem – 17
  Stimulating widespread prosperity
    – 46
Skill, and knowledge – 58, 59, 61
Slavery – 84, 85
Smith, Adam
  Criticized by Henry George on
    selfishness - 54
Smith, Jeff
  On corporate charters – 39
  The Protestant Work Ethic vs the
    Polynesian Play Ethic – 55-56
Social development – 60
Social Problems
  Henry George quoted on popular
    government – 20
Socialist – 23
Statistics
  Use of, in over-population debate
    – 11
Subsistence – 54

Sullivan, Mark A.
  Preface – 6-8
Sustainable production – 76
Taxation
  Abolish all except upon land
    values – 7
  Cutting – 87
  Rates – 87
Terminology
  Debates over – 48
Thatcher, Margaret
  Tax-cutting regime - 87
The Land Question
  Quoted on law of development as
  law of integration – 44-45
The Mason Gaffney Reader – 7, 117
The Sassafras Crossing – 112, 113,
  114
The Science of Political Economy – 10,
  30, 53, 54, 58, 69, 75, 77, 115
  Quoted – 30, 31, 51, 52
Tideman, Nicolaus – 96
"Tragedy of the Commons" – 65
Uehara, Osamu – 8
Understanding Economics – 10, 115
Unemployment, involuntary – 55
United Labor Party
  Henry George's mayoral
  campaign of 1886 – 20
Value
  Austrian theory of – 26-28
  From obligation – 29
  Henry George's view: a function
  of buyers' desires – 28-29
  In production or obligation - 42
  Labor-saved theory of – 62
  Labor theory of – 24-26, 28, 29,
  52, 53
  Subjective – 62
  Surplus, in Marxist analysis – 25,
  88
Value Added Tax (VAT)
  Use in Bangladesh - 104, 105

Village Gate, The – 112
Vincent, Joshua – 8
Virtual Frontier – 63-71
Voting – 21, 22
Wage slavery – 57
Wages
  Paid to producers less than earned
  - 88
  Produced by labor – 14
Wages-Fund Theory refuted by
  Henry George – 14
Walton, Sue – 8
"Want and fear of want" – 55
War
  No such thing as an honorable
  war – 17
  Single Tax a solution – 17
  Spending diverts financial
  resources from societal needs - 18
Warren, Elizabeth – 92
Wealth
  And services – 50, 74, 75
  Defined in The Science of Political
  Economy – 51-52
Websites created by Lindy Davies –
  114
  (See Index of Online References,
  below)
White, John Z.
  Corporate charter is not a
  contract - 38
  "Dartmouth College Decision" of
  the US Supreme Court – 37-40
Wildlife habitat – 93
Wilson, Woodrow – 20
Zarlenga, Stephen – 91

Online References

Earthsharing.org – 105
harrison-moore-apbQ77SBWiE-unsplash.jpg – 106
http://www.ecinlib.org/library/ricardo/ricP.html – 61
http://paidcontent.org/article/419-akamais-patent-lawsuit-likely-to-be-a-
    giantheadache-for-startup-cotend/
http://www.progress.org/archive/fold198.htm – 41
http://www.progress.org/archive/hgjr25c.htm – 41
http://www.progress.org/archive/subsidy01.htm – 41
http://www.progress.org/authors/lindy-davies – 110

Websites created by Lindy Davies – 114

http://www.henrygeorge.org
http://landreform.org/bob/
http://truefreetrade.org/
http://politicaleconomy.org/
http://www.georgistjournal.org/
http://www.masongaffneyreader.com/
http://prosperidad.org/

Did you enjoy reading Lindy Davies and the
Georgist Journal?
Would you like to pursue these ideas further?
Here are some possible next steps.

Take our course in Political Economy

Henry George Institute offers distance-learning courses via the
Internet and regular mail. Our three-course series in *Principles of
Political Economy* includes *Understanding Economics*; *Applied
Economics: Globalization and Trade*; and *Economic Science*. The
courses may be taken separately, but together they provide a
comprehensive overview of basic economic theory and issues.
Courses may be taken on one's own, or with feedback from an
HGI instructor. These courses can be found at:
www.henrygeorge.org

Join the Henry George Institute

Joining HGI is an opportunity to engage with others who look
at Economics from the thoughtful and compassionate point of
view as found in Lindy Davies' essays. Members are eligible to
vote in the annual election for the Board of Directors and to
volunteer and assist HGI's programs. Dues are just $20 (US
Dollars) per year; and additional donations are most welcome.

Our Statement of Purpose and Who We Are

In accordance with the philosophy of Henry George, the Henry George Institute holds that all persons have a right to the use of the earth and that all have a right to the fruits of their labor. To implement these rights it is proposed that the rent of land be taken by the community as public revenue, and that all taxes on labor and the fruits of labor be abolished. The Institute believes with George that "liberty means justice and justice is the natural law," and that the social and economic ills besetting the world today are the result of non-conformance to natural law. The Institute pledges itself to bring this philosophy to the attention of the public by all suitable means.

Henry George Institute is incorporated as a non-profit educational organization in New York State, and a recognized charity pursuant to the US Internal Revenue Code 501(c)(3). American donations are tax-deductible. Founded in 1971 as a membership organization, HGI is supported by dues, contributions, and volunteer participation. If you agree that the philosophy of Henry George has important answers to today's urgent problems, consider joining and supporting the Institute. Thank you.

Our office address is: HGI, 4075 Cheltonham Ct., Plainfield, IN 46168; Our website is: www.henrygeorge.org; our email address is: info@henrygeorge.org

Find us on Facebook
https://www.facebook.com/understandecon/

Made in the USA
Middletown, DE
24 July 2022

69948058R00069